MW00353377

"In this provocative book, Flood exposes the grave deficiencies of the penal substitution model of atonement, pinpointing its shallow treatment of the depth and the gravity of sin . . . Armed with astute interpretations of Scripture, he focuses on the love of God and reinterprets justice as restorative . . . Finally, after centuries of suffering under a legal perception of atonement, Flood has shown us that the good news is truly good news!"

—**Sharon L. Baker,**
author of *Razing Hell*

"On a cresting wave of reaction against violent atonement theory, *Healing the Gospel* charts a sea-change course back to Jesus's ministry as a model of gracious restoration, moving far beyond the traditional, abusive contours of penal substitution as explanation of Christ's death . . . Jesus dies to show us God's enemy-love, which changes everything. A splendid, stirring, and essential book!"

—**Anthony Bartlett,**
author of *Cross Purposes*

"Anyone concerned about the connection between theology and violence in American society will welcome Flood's *Healing the Gospel*. In a readable format, he explains why we should abandon violence-accommodating, penal substitutionary atonement, and replace it with atonement imagery that reflects the restorative justice Jesus lived."

—**J. Denny Weaver,**
author of *The Nonviolent Atonement*

Healing the Gospel

Healing the Gospel

A Radical Vision for Grace, Justice, and the Cross

DEREK FLOOD

Foreword by
BRIAN D. MCLAREN

CASCADE *Books* • Eugene, Oregon

HEALING THE GOSPEL
A Radical Vision for Grace, Justice, and the Cross

Copyright © 2012 Derek Flood. All rights reserved. Except for brief quotations in critical publications or reviews, no part of this book may be reproduced in any manner without prior written permission from the publisher. Write: Permissions, Wipf and Stock Publishers, 199 W. 8th Ave., Suite 3, Eugene, OR 97401.

Cascade Books
An Imprint of Wipf and Stock Publishers
199 W. 8th Ave., Suite 3
Eugene, OR 97401

www.wipfandstock.com

ISBN 13: 978-1-4982-1528-2

All scripture quotations, unless otherwise indicated, are taken from the THE HOLY BIBLE, NEW INTERNATIONAL VERSION®, NIV® Copyright © 1973, 1978, 1984, 2011 by Biblica, Inc.™ Used by permission. All rights reserved worldwide.

Illustrations by Derek Flood.

Cataloging-in-Publication data:

Flood, Derek.

Healing the gospel : a radical vision for grace, justice, and the cross / Derek Flood.

xiv + 120 p. ; 23 cm. —Includes bibliographical references.

ISBN 13: 978-1-4982-1528-2

1. Atonement. 2. Jesus Christ—Crucifixion. I. Title.

BT265.2 .F56 2012

Manufactured in the U.S.A.

In memory of Walter Wink (1935–2012)

CONTENTS

FOREWORD

FOR ME, GROWING UP evangelical meant growing up believing that the gospel *was* the theory of penal substitutionary atonement. Trusting Christ, accepting Christ, getting saved, being born again all meant—covertly or overtly—accepting the doctrine of penal substitutionary atonement, namely, that God's justice requires that we all be sent to hell forever, but that God punished his perfect son Jesus in our place, which means we can go to heaven.

That's the version of the gospel that is broadcast 24/7 on radio and television across America, around the world. That's the version of the gospel that many missionaries use to define effectiveness, that many theologians use to define faithfulness, and that many Christians and non-Christians alike use to define Christianity itself.

Given how deeply rooted this understanding of the gospel is (especially in evangelical, charismatic, and even some Roman Catholic circles), it's no wonder that I couldn't imagine questioning it for most of my life. Penal substitutionary atonement was the heart of the gospel! The whole system of Christianity would be frivolous, meaningless, or ridiculous without it!

Then came a conversation with a well-known evangelical theologian who asked me a simple question: shouldn't we let Jesus define the gospel? That question forced me to take seriously Jesus' gospel—the good news of the kingdom of God, here and available now to all who repent and believe. What did Jesus mean by kingdom of God? How did that relate to my inherited understanding of the atonement?

Those questions disrupted my system, but that only meant I had to fit my cherished atonement theory in a new place—maybe not at the center of the gospel, but certainly in an important footnote position.

Then came another conversation with another well-known evangelical theologian, a few years later. He was asked what parts of evangelical theology needed to be re-thought, and without a heartbeat of hesitation, his first of three replies was "the doctrine of atonement." What?

That sent me on a long process of rethinking. I started asking questions that made a lot of my friends nervous.

And back then, there was no book like this one by Derek Flood to help me. But now there is such a book to help you.

You may never have even heard the precise term "penal substitutionary atonement," but you "know" it—it's the point of everything for millions of Christians around the world. The only problem that really matters? God's just and infinite wrath at our sin. The only good news that really matters? How to be rescued from falling into that fiery lake of divine wrath. The main reason Jesus matters? Because he took that wrath upon himself so we don't have to.

If you've begun to have qualms about some parts of that doctrinal system, this is the book you need. I'm enthusiastic about it for four reasons.

First, it's simple and short. True, many of the ideas in this book can be found in thick and nearly impenetrable theological tomes. But no book focuses on the question of what's wrong with conventional penal substitutionary atonement theory better than this one—in a slim and readable book, and in terms and syntax that any literate person can understand.

Second, it engages with Scripture in a responsible, mature, and faithful way. From his reading of Romans to his reading of Isaiah 53, from his insights into Paul to his insights into Jesus, from his engagement with specific biblical terms (like *justice, sin, saving,* and *wrath*) to his understanding of the general biblical narrative, Derek models how to make good biblical and theological scholarship accessible to normal folks.

Third, this book engages with Christian history with equal maturity, responsibility, and faithfulness. He brings ancient voices like Athanasius and Gregory into conversation with contemporary ones like Wink, Girard, and Sittser. Where he must disagree—whether with historic figures like Anselm or contemporary ones like Packer—he does so respectfully, sympathetically, and fairly, not rudely, rashly, or dismissively.

And fourth, this book combines the mind of a theologian with the eye and heart of an artist. Derek sees that meaning comes in images and narratives, not just in formulas, theories, or models. So he combines the two, and in the process, presents us with something we thought we knew but didn't really.

No doubt that's a big part of what *repentance* means . . . acknowledging that we didn't really know before, and thereby opening ourselves up to a fresh and deeper knowing.

I had two great fears when I began rethinking my inherited understanding of the gospel and the atonement. First, I was afraid that I would get in trouble with my authority figures and peers: I lived in circles where honest difference of opinion on such matters was not easily tolerated. Second, I was afraid that I would end up somewhere that was less biblical than where I started. Because I didn't have a book available to me like this one, I stepped out with great fear and trembling.

But as I read Derek's book, I feel more than ever that the view he proposes is not less biblically defensible, and not even equally so, but far more so. I think you'll agree that the view he proposes is most faithful to Scripture in its totality, both in a close reading where all the details are attended to, and in a more expansive reading for the broader themes and narratives that it explores.

This fresh approach to the Bible not only heals our understanding of the gospel, but it also offers healing to us—because a distorted gospel will inevitably harm us. And through us, a distorted gospel harms the world at large.

Our world suffers not only from the ravages of sin—personal and systemic, but also from the ravages of sincere and zealous but misguided and misguiding religion. This book, like the original gospel it seeks to clarify, is about being saved, freed, and healed from all those ravages, in all their forms.

That's why I am so grateful for this book. If you are willing to step out and walk through the following pages with Derek Flood as your guide, a lot of healing can flow. A lot of healing indeed.

Brian D. McLaren

ACKNOWLEDGMENTS

THEOLOGY IS ALWAYS A collaborative work. Listening to the struggles and stories in the many emails and comments I received over the years from readers of my blog (including those who have disagreed with me) has helped shape this book in a profound way, and I am grateful for all those conversations.

I'd like to thank everyone who read through the manuscript and proposal in its many drafts along the way—to Bucky Rosenbaum for your invaluable insights into the world of publishing, to Brian McLaren and Mark Baker for your support and encouragement from the very beginning, to Michael Gorman for relentlessly pushing me towards scholarly excellence, to Josh Rowley for your eagle eye for detail, to my professors at the Graduate Theological Union, especially my thesis committee: Ted Peters and Greg Love, as well as my Greek professors Gary Pence and Everett Kalin.

I wish to thank my editor Rodney Clapp and all the good folks at Wipf and Stock. In a publishing world increasingly driven solely by profit, your commitment to judging books based on their merit truly puts you on the cutting edge of Christian publishing, and I'm proud to be a small part of that with you.

Most of all, I owe a great debt of gratitude to my wife Julia Flood, whose insights as a psychotherapist have profoundly shaped my theology and understanding of our human condition. She has read countless drafts, and sat through my endless early morning theological rants, understanding my mind, but more than that, knowing my heart. So while the title bears my name, she is there on every line.

1

THE LIMITS OF LAW

Penal Substitution and the Failure of Retributive Justice

WHEN I WAS A teenager I had the typical born again experience, complete with all the strong emotions and tears. Only it wasn't typical at all for me. I had not been raised in church. I was an agnostic, and so had always assumed that God was just an idea in your head. So to feel God's loving presence, to hear that still small voice telling me, over and over again, that I was loved, that I was not alone, was simply earth shattering for me. I can hardly express how profoundly it changed me to experience being loved by God like that. It turned my whole world around.

Naturally, I wanted to share this with everyone I met, so when they handed out tracts for us to distribute and told us how to "share the gospel" at my church, I was the first in line. Only, I quickly discovered that the message I was taught to share with others was very different from what I had actually experienced. It seemed more like bad news, and led to all sorts of awkward conversations like this:

Jesus died for you!

Why did Jesus have to die?

Because of our sin.

What if we haven't sinned?

"All have sinned and fallen short of the glory of God." No one can keep the law.

But if no one can keep it how can we be blamed for that?

Because "the wages of sin is death" and so justice requires that you be sent to be tormented in Hell for all eternity.

That's awful!

Yes, but there's good news: God has provided a way out by sacrificing his Son.

God kills his own son?

Yes, that's how much he loves you.

Why would that make anything better?

Because it satisfies God's need for punishment. Sin must be paid for with blood because "without blood there is no forgiveness."

I feel ill.

Can't you see this is God's mercy and love? Don't you want to open your heart and let him into your life?

I think I have to go now.

The above dialog is of course overplayed in order to drive home this simple point: The way many of us have learned to present the "good news" can sound like anything *but* good news. I had experienced God's overwhelming love and grace filling my life. Yet I was taught to tell people that they *deserved* to be punished by God forever. Taught that we should see ourselves as *worthless, totally depraved, capable of nothing good* apart from God. I was taught that the reason Jesus died was because God demanded that someone had to suffer the penalty of sin, someone had to be punished to appease God's wrath. No wonder I got a cold shoulder when I tried to share this "good news" with people.

Countless people filling our pews have internalized this hurtful view of God and themselves. Roberta Bondi recalls the revival meetings at Pond Fork Baptist Church in Kentucky she attended each summer as a child:

> The goal of a revival was to create or revive in everybody the three-fold conviction that each of us was so rotten to the core that we deserved to die and roast in hell forever; that God was enraged at us enough to kill us; and finally, that, in spite of everything, God

loved us enough to rescue us by sending his son as a sacrifice to die in our place.[1]

Bondi goes on to tell how this led her to internalize a sense of self-loathing that robbed her of joy. It is the kind of shame, she says, that "consumes you with anger, that renders you passive, that swallows you in depression, that keeps you from loving and knowing yourself to be loved."[2] Faith motivated by fear, threat, and feelings of worthlessness. Her story is, sadly, not uncommon.

This kind of religious self-loathing is often expressed as pious devotion: "I feel myself to be a lump of unworthiness, a mass of corruption, and a heap of sin, apart from His almighty love."[3] These are the words of Charles Spurgeon, a preacher who genuinely intended these words to be understood as an expression of love and gratitude towards God. People offer such prayers thinking this is what the Bible says about them, and believing that it is what God wants to hear us say. But consider for a moment how you would feel if your own child said such things to you: It would devastate you to hear your own son or daughter speak of themselves this way, and all the more to know that this is what your child thought *you wanted to hear*. If we as parents would feel this way about our children, how much more would it break God's heart to hear us say such things? Isn't God the father who runs out to meet the prodigal son? Isn't God the one who loved us even in our estranged state?

How could things have gone so wrong? When did the good news become bad news? Behind all of this lies an image of God as a judge who is primarily concerned with satisfaction of punitive justice. This is the image of God that plagued sixteenth-century reformer Martin Luther with the horrible sense that he could never be good enough. The weight of this became so pronounced that at one point he confesses bitterly, "I did not love, and in fact I hated that righteous God who punished sinners . . . I was angry with God . . . I drove myself mad with a desperate disturbed conscience."[4]

It is not insignificant that Luther's own father and mother were both harsh disciplinarians, but regardless of the cause, Luther had clearly internalized a crippling image of God as judge that tormented him until he discovered grace. This message of grace and forgiveness has been a life-changing

1. Bondi, *Memories of God*, 116.

2. Ibid., 144.

3. Spurgeon, *All of Grace*, 6.

4. Quoted in McGrath, *Luther's Theology of the Cross*, 97.

one to many people over the ages since Luther rediscovered it, but it has often been tragically accompanied by a message of fear and condemnation itself. Luther, for example, preached that one must face the horrors of wrath before one could come to grace. In other words, he believed that everyone needed to be forced to go through the horrible struggle he did before they could hear about grace.

Ever since then, there has been a long history of revival preachers who have proclaimed this "pre-gospel" of fear, threat, and condemnation—telling people the bad news so they could then receive the good news, wounding people first, so they could then heal those wounds. The philosophy behind this strategy is that people need to be shaken out of their complacency and made ready to respond to the gospel.

This may indeed be true for some, but for others it amounts to little more than abuse, and has resulted in a hurtful image of God being hammered into their heads that has estranged them from God, and driven them away from faith. For a person struggling with moral failure, facing up to their brokenness and realizing that God loves them and died for them despite it is a crucial step towards life. But to tell a person whose sin is self-hatred that they need to face how bad and worthless they are is like making them swallow the wrong prescription medicine—what was healing to the first person, is poison to the second.

For people like Luther, Bunyan, or Wesley (all of whom have deeply shaped the character of evangelicalism), I would suggest that their true struggle was not one of guilt at all. Their problem was not the petty infractions they would constantly accuse themselves of (Wesley, for example, after doing some good deed for the poor, would often condemn himself for feeling pleased about it[5]). No, their real struggle was with the devastation done to their souls through self-loathing masquerading as piety.

So they struggled with their feelings of shame and worthlessness, desperately longing for grace, longing for God's assurance and love, yet continuing to assume that their broken view of an angry, condemning, punishing God was the correct view, the biblical view. What I want to propose is that this is not in fact what the New Testament teaches at all.

---

5. An example is Wesley's sermon Number 14, "Repentance of Believers" I.12–13, "When they are comforting the afflicted, or provoking one another to love and to good works, do they never perceive any inward self-commendation: 'Now you have spoken well?' . . . So that they are now more ashamed of their best duties, than they were once of their worst sins."

A HISTORY OF VIOLENCE

For centuries the assumption of punitive justice has saturated nearly every segment of our Western society—shaping how we approached child rearing, education, mental health, and of course our criminal justice system. It was common in the past for instance to think it was good to beat children at home and at school, or to beat one's servants and workers.

Over the last century however, there have been major shifts in how we understand justice and its relation to punishment. Far from being good for a person's soul, today we have increasingly come to realize that such violence instead can cause significant psychological damage that stunts a person's healthy development. As I am writing this for example, the Twitter universe is exploding with the shocking story of school officials who put an autistic boy in a closed gym bag and left him in the hallway to discipline him. People across the country are understandably outraged, but this is exactly the kind of thing that we used to do to people all the time, believing that inflicting this kind of discipline would "make him come to his senses." The outrage people express now reflects the broad shift throughout our society away from that punitive model.

One of the last places where we still embrace the idea of punitive justice today is in our prison systems. Yet even within the criminal justice system there is an increasing awareness that a strictly punitive approach rarely produces reform. Offenders who simply serve their time commonly go right back out and commit more crimes because the root factors have not been dealt with. In fact, the violent environment of our prison system becomes a breeding ground that turns petty offenders into hardened criminals. Rather than learning empathy and how to manage their impulses and emotions, the brutal culture of prison life teaches people that one must be brutally violent in order to survive. Because of these patterns learned in prison, the alarming repeat offense rate is sadly not at all surprising. Locking someone up in the hell of prison life naturally breeds violence, not reform or repentance.[6]

People do not learn empathy by being shamed and dehumanized. On the contrary, developing empathy has a lot to do with a healthy sense of self-worth. So while we may feel an impulse to want to punish and hurt those who have hurt us, this does not mend the hurt, it simply perpetuates it. In other words, punishment and shame are not the solution, they are a

6. See Zehr, *Changing Lenses*.

part of the problem. Punitive justice does not make things better, it makes them worse.

As a society we are increasingly coming to realize this. Across the broad fields of child rearing, education, and mental health (and slowly within the criminal justice system as well) there has been a major shift over the last half-century away from a punitive model, and towards a restorative one. Towards a model that fosters empathy, restoration, and healing.

TWO KINDS OF JUSTICE

While our understanding of justice has shifted as a society away from a punitive model and towards a restorative one, most of us continue to think that punitive justice is what the Bible teaches. As a result, many Christians defend a punitive model, even when it conflicts with their own values. As the painful testimonies of Bondi and so many others illustrate: We struggle to believe it, even though it seems wrong and hurtful to us. We hate it, but think this is what God wants us to believe.

More specifically, we think that the gospel is rooted in the idea that Jesus had to die to fulfill the "demands" of (punitive) justice. This is an understanding of the atonement known as *penal substitution*, "penal" meaning punish, and "substitution" meaning that Jesus is punished instead of us. It is the most common understanding of the atonement today.

Penal substitution classically sees a conflict between God's desire for mercy (which in this legal framework refers to God's desire to be lenient and not punish), and the demand for justice (which it sees as focused on punishment). In this view, love is viewed as sentimental, weak, and opposed to justice. It represents leniency and inaction. God wants to be lenient, but justice requires punishment. So Jesus is punished in our place, fulfilling the demands of justice and appeasing God's anger.

What I want to propose is that the above is not at all what the Bible teaches, and instead is the result of people projecting their worldly understanding of punitive justice onto the biblical text. The New Testament, in contrast, is actually a *critique* of punitive justice. It presents it as a problem to be solved, not as the means to the solution. The problem of wrath (that is, punitive justice) is *overcome* through the cross, which is an act of restoration—restoring humanity to a right relationship with God. In other words, restorative justice is how God in Christ acts to heal the problem of punitive justice.

Love is not in conflict with justice, love is how justice comes about because the New Testament understanding of justice is ultimately not about punishment, but about *making things right again*. After his book length study of biblical justice, Chris Marshall concludes, "The justice of God is not primarily or normatively a retributive justice or a distributive justice but a restorative or reconstructive justice, a saving action by God that recreates shalom and makes things right."[7]

This is not simply one theme found in Scripture, it is *the* core narrative of the gospel—the master story of God in Christ reconciling the world to himself (2 Cor 5:19). It is the story of restoration, redemption—at-one-ment. This meta-narrative of redemption is rooted, as Marshall says, in the idea of *restorative justice*. That is, justice understood in terms of God in Christ restoring and making things right again.

Restorative justice comes *through* mercy because it has to do with acting to make things right. In contrast, the model of punitive justice—which penal substitution is based on—reflects an understanding of both justice and mercy that is in conflict with the vision of the New Testament. In the following chart we can see the two contrasting models of justice side by side:

Criminal Model	New Testament Model
Justice = punishing	Justice = making things right
Mercy = leniency and inaction	Mercy = the act of making things right
Mercy and justice are in conflict	Acts of mercy are the means to justice

Biblical mercy means active *compassion*, not inactive leniency. It is not about closing our eyes to sin and suffering, but just the opposite: Jesus had compassion for sinners not because he was denying their sin but precisely because he *did* see, and their estranged plight agonized Jesus. Because of that compassion Jesus longed to bring them justice, to release the oppressed, heal the afflicted, and forgive the condemned. Restorative justice likewise is rooted in compassion and reflects a desire to see things made right, to see relationships restored, to see broken lives mended, to see hurtful and hurting people come to their knees in repentance and be made new.

7. Marshall, *Beyond Retribution*, 53.

CONCLUSION

As we have seen, punitive justice has had devastating effects on many people's lives, leading to all sorts of hurt over the centuries (beating children, torturing prisoners and heretics, etc.) and producing a deeply hurtful understanding of who we are and who God is. In contrast, I have argued for adopting a restorative understanding of justice. This restorative model not only reflects a major shift in how our society as a whole has come to think, but is also the core narrative of the New Testament.

However, centuries of projecting our cultural assumptions of punitive justice onto the Bible are not easy to shake off. It has become so ingrained, so indoctrinated, into our religious imagination that it seems self-evident. Therefore, we will need to take a fresh look at Scripture in order to recognize this model of restorative justice at the heart of the biblical narrative. This will be the focus of the next chapter.

2

GOD'S JUSTICE

Restorative Justice as the Heart of the Gospel

CENTURIES OF READING THE Bible through the culturally dominant lens of punitive justice are hard to shake off. We read the word "justice" in our Bibles and simply assume that it is referring to punitive justice. But if we can manage to take a fresh look at scripture, and in particular the New Testament, what we will find is that the master narrative of the Bible—God's salvation in Jesus that all of scripture points towards—is rooted in a model of restorative justice.

As a case in point, let's consider the book of Romans, which has long been considered to be Paul's masterpiece, and one of the clearest articulations of the Christian gospel. A traditional Lutheran reading of Romans understands Paul to be addressing the problem of a guilty conscience: How can guilty sinners facing God's wrath instead find a gracious God?

As important and valid as Luther's questions may have been in his own context, recent scholarship has drawn attention to the fact that this is not at all Paul's point. That is, Paul is not addressing people who wanted (like Luther) to escape God's wrath and judgment. Quite to the contrary, Paul is addressing people who are crying out *for* judgment, who longed for God to come in wrath and punish sinners. Paul is addressing a religious audience that has embraced the idea of punitive or retributive justice, and arguing *against* their perspective. In other words, Paul's argument in

Romans is that righteousness comes through restorative justice *instead of* retributive justice.

Paul begins in the first chapter of Romans by painting a picture of pagan cultic worship that would have been seen as appalling to his audience. One can imagine them fervently nodding in approval when Paul says that God's wrath is coming because of this, thinking, "Those hated Gentile outsiders are finally going to get what they have coming!" But then Paul suddenly turns the tables on his religious audience in chapter two, declaring "You, therefore, have no excuse, you who pass judgment on someone else" (Rom 2:1), challenging his audience's tendency towards self-righteous judgmentalism, and pointing out their own hypocrisy. They have no room to judge because they are just as guilty, Paul says. If they want to point fingers, that same way of judgment and condemnation will come right back at them. This all brings us to a pivotal passage in Paul's argument. I'll quote the whole section at length, and then we can come back and look at each part in more detail:

> But now apart from the law the righteousness of God has been made known, to which the Law and the Prophets testify. This righteousness is given through faith in Jesus Christ to all who believe. There is no difference between Jew and Gentile, for all have sinned and fall short of the glory of God, and all are justified freely by his grace through the redemption that came by Christ Jesus. God presented Christ as a sacrifice of atonement, through the shedding of his blood—to be received by faith. He did this to demonstrate his righteousness, because in his forbearance he had left the sins committed beforehand unpunished—he did it to demonstrate his righteousness at the present time, so as to be just and the one who justifies those who have faith in Jesus. (Rom 3:21–26)

To understand the context here, lets begin by looking at verse 25, where Paul says that God chose the cross in order to "demonstrate his righteousness, because in his forbearance he had left the sins committed beforehand unpunished." The New Living Translation puts it like this: "This sacrifice shows that God was being fair when he held back and did not punish those who sinned in times past." In other words, in the eyes of his Jewish audience, God's *not* judging and punishing sin was seen as unjust. As a people long in exile, living under pagan oppression, they *wanted* God to come in wrath and judge the Gentile sinners. God judging sin meant for them that the victims would be avenged. So when God did not come in wrath, this seemed in their eyes to be unjust.

In a similar vein, many people today think that not punishing means ignoring hurtful behavior. People therefore speak of being "soft on crime," implying that the only alternative to harsh sentencing is letting crime run rampant. Others advocate corporal punishment of children, claiming that one must choose between being a harsh disciplinarian or an unengaged laissez-faire parent whose children run wild. In this limited perspective, one either punishes, or one turns a blind eye to injustice.

Paul is advocating a third way that is neither violent retribution nor inaction—the way of restoration. Paul's religious audience believed that if God was just, God would punish. Paul instead says that God is "just and the one who justifies sinners" (v. 26). In other words, God is indeed just and demonstrates this by making sinners whole again. Justice does not come through punishment and violence, but through restoration.

A VIOLENT MAN

With that context in mind, let's return to our passage which begins, "But now apart from the law the righteousness of God has been made known" (Rom 3:21). Paul is contrasting two opposing ways of bringing about justice. On the one hand we have punitive justice, rooted in the law's system of reward and punishment, blessings and curses, which his audience has embraced. Paul contrasts that with what he calls "the righteousness of God." The Greek word translated here as "righteousness" can also be rendered as "justice." So we could also translate this as "*God's justice* has been made known." It's important to note however that the term refers to a justice rooted in God's *goodness*. Hence, N.T. Wright defines this "righteousness/ justice from God" as "the instrument of putting the world to rights—what we might call cosmic restorative justice."[1] What Paul calls "God's justice" is restorative justice.

Beginning in chapter two, Paul has been criticizing the assumptions of his religious audience who are calling out for justice in the form of retribution and punishment. Now he proposes that God's justice really comes through God's action in Christ to restore all of humanity in love. Restorative justice instead of punitive justice.

Paul's original audience was not struggling with a guilty conscience, they were religious people who had adopted what Walter Wink has called "the myth of redemptive violence" as the means of bringing about justice,

1. Wright, "Letter to the Romans," 400.

and were struggling with feeling that God was unjust in not coming in wrath. Paul is arguing against that view of justice, saying it leads to death and condemnation, and instead proclaiming God's superior way of restorative justice in Christ.

Paul then goes on to explain how God's restorative justice in Christ comes about: God acts in Christ to make us good. A key concept here is "justification" which normally refers to legal acquittal, i.e., declaring a person innocent in court, and has often been mistranslated as such in Romans. But if that were the case then Paul's entire argument would fall apart. He is arguing that it was just for God not to punish sinners as his audience wished. If his only reason was that God had declared these sinners to be innocent, this would have been seen by his audience as a profound injustice—the acquittal of the guilty. Read within the larger context of his argument in Romans we can see that Paul instead is creatively re-appropriating the term in its literal sense to mean "*making* righteous."[2] God brings about true justice, Paul tells us, by making sinners into saints. This act of redemptive transformation is nothing short of a miracle and happens through relationship—through being loved by God, and God's goodness making us good. Paul goes on to explain in Romans 7–8 that as God's Spirit indwells us, as we experience Christ's indwelling love, we are relationally transformed into his likeness. This way of the Spirit brings life, Paul says, but the way of law (i.e., the way of retributive justice) brings death.

Now, Paul's critique of the law is well known. Recent scholarship has helpfully drawn attention to the fact that Paul is not opposing good works here (i.e., acts of love and mercy) as a typical Lutheran reading would claim, rather Paul is ultimately arguing *for* works of love. This "new perspective on Paul," as it is called, stresses that both Jesus and Paul saw fulfillment of the law as embodied in compassion rather than in legal ritualistic observance.[3] But if that is all there is to it—if all he is saying is that love takes priority over ritual—why does Paul get so completely livid about this? Why does he look back and call all the things he used to be so proud of from that way "garbage" (Phil 3:8), and declare anyone who follows it to be "under a curse" (Gal 3:10)?

I want to suggest that one major reason is that Paul is not simply rejecting ritual, he is rejecting the inherent violence found in that way. Note

2. See the appendix for a detailed study of this reading of justification in Romans, and its relation to the "justice of God" in Paul's thought.

3. Dunn, *Jesus, Paul and the Law*, 28.

how the specific sins Paul accuses his religious audience of here in Romans all have to do with malice and violence:

> Their throats are open graves; their tongues practice deceit.
> The poison of vipers is on their lips.
> Their mouths are full of cursing and bitterness.
> Their feet are swift to shed blood;
> ruin and misery mark their ways,
> and the way of peace they do not know. (Rom 3:13–17)

This is not just an accusation, it is a confession, reflecting Paul's former religious life. Paul was not a sinner who "got religion." Paul was already religious, in fact he was a religious zealot who could boast that his observance of the Torah was "faultless" (Phil 3:6). Yet despite this, Paul came to regard himself as "the worst of all sinners" and "a violent man" (1 Tim 1:13, 15). He confesses painfully, "I do not even deserve to be called an apostle, because I persecuted the church of God" (1 Cor 15:9). That's why Pauline scholar James Dunn describes Paul's conversion as a conversion *away from* religion characterized by "zealous and violent hostility."[4]

In other words, Paul's great sin, as he came to see it, had been participation in what he understood as religiously justified acts of violence motivated by religious zeal. His conversion was a conversion away from the religiously justified violence he had formally embraced. It was not a rejection of his Jewish faith (Paul continued to regard himself as a faithful Jew), rather it was a recognition that his former embrace of violence in God's name was not in fact an act of faithfulness, but a grave sin.

Now to be sure, one does indeed find the idea of retributive justice in the Bible. In fact, this was precisely how Paul had read his Bible before he encountered Christ. Before his conversion, Paul had read his Bible and concluded that he should commit violence in God's name. He was convinced that justice comes through punishment, and saw himself as an agent of that. After his encounter with Christ on the road to Damascus, Paul completely reassessed how to understand scripture, leading him to a radically different understanding focused on God's way of restorative justice in Christ. Now Paul is trying to get his readers to see that, too. Paul has converted away from the way of retribution, and Romans is his treatise explaining why the way of restorative justice is a better way.

---

4. Dunn, *Theology of Paul the Apostle*, 353.

THE PERFECT LAW-BREAKER

Having looked at Paul's conversion from retributive justice to restorative justice, and his proclamation of that in Romans, let's take a look at Jesus and how he related to the law.

Proponents of penal substitution portray Jesus as the perfect law-keeper. Yet the presentation we see of Jesus in the Gospels gives us a very different picture: In the Gospels Jesus is frequently accused of breaking the law. He breaks the Sabbath regulations to heal (Luke 6:7–11); touches the unclean, thus making himself unclean (compare Mark 5:25–43 with Lev 15:19); and practices table fellowship with sinners (Mark 2:15; Matt 9:10; Luke 5:29; Luke 15:2). Because of all this, he is accused of being a drunk, a blasphemer, a "friend of sinners," and even in league with the devil (Luke 7:34; 5:21; 7:34; 11:15). In short, Jesus is not presented as a model law-keeper in the Gospels at all, but rather as one who scandalized the keepers of the law, frequently coming into open confrontation with them.

Now, Jesus did not see his actions as being unfaithful to God. He argued that he was actually fulfilling the law in doing all these things. Yet in faithfully acting to restore people, the Gospel writers tell us, Jesus continually *appeared* in the eyes of the religious leaders around him to be breaking God's laws. In short, his focus was in showing love and compassion to those in need, even if that meant being judged as a lawbreaker. He prioritized people over rules.[5]

Jesus often sought out these confrontations. On one occasion he has a man with a shriveled hand stand up in front of everyone in the synagogue, and then asks, "which is lawful on the Sabbath: to do good or to do evil, to save life or to destroy it?" (Luke 6:9). Jesus looks around, but no one answers. Finally Jesus, clearly upset, says to the man, "stretch out your hand" and heals him in front of everyone (v. 10). Luke tells us that this open confrontation made the Pharisees and the teachers of the law "furious" (v. 11).

Why would Jesus do this? Why would he defiantly break commandments, infuriating the religious leaders and keepers of the law? Couldn't he have waited until Monday to heal him? In fact, they ask him this very question, "There are six days for work. So come and be healed on those days, not on the Sabbath" (Luke 13:14). Jesus refuses to wait one more day. In fact, he asks, what better day is there to heal than the Lord's day (v. 15)? Of course he could have waited a day and avoided any confrontation. The

---

5. See Loader, *Jesus and the Fundamentalism of His Day*, 138–46.

fact is, he was deliberately courting confrontation because he saw how toxic religion was hurting people, and was calling them on it.

This was not a confrontation between Judaism and Christianity. Jesus was a Jew. What we see throughout the Gospels is a confrontation between faith that works to bring life, and faith that crushes life. As we saw in the last chapter, this same type of toxic religion is alive and well today in our own churches. And it is crushing people today just as it did then. That made Jesus really mad.

This is dramatically captured in his haunting rebuke "woe unto you, teachers of the law" (Matt 23:13). Jesus is opposed to their "law-keeping" because it hurt people, pushing them away from God. Jesus acts to restore people and refuses to be held back by legal restrictions, but they do the opposite and "shut the door of the kingdom of heaven in people's faces" (v. 13). As a result, Jesus tells them, they completely miss what really matters: acting in compassion and restorative justice (v. 23).

The portrait that the Gospel writers want to give us of Jesus—who they affirmed as being the embodiment of holiness—was not of a model law keeper. On the contrary they repeatedly show us that the reputation Jesus had among the proponents of the law was of a law breaker defying the demands of the temple and religious authority, and associating himself not with the righteous but with sinners.

Jesus' entire ministry of healing the sick, caring for the poor, and forgiving sinners can be said to be a demonstration of restorative justice. The hallmark of his moral teaching—love of enemies—likewise acts to overturn the way of retributive justice with restorative justice: "You have heard that it was said, 'Eye for eye, and tooth for tooth.' But I tell you, do not resist an evil person" (Matt 5:38–39). "You have heard that it was said, 'Love your neighbor and hate your enemy.' But I tell you: Love your enemies and pray for those who persecute you" (vv. 43–44).

Many have pointed out that the Mosaic legislation calling for "an eye for an eye" itself acted to curb the escalation of retributive violence, limiting it to just *one* eye for an eye instead of the 7 for Cain (Gen 4:15), and then the 77 of Lamech (Gen 4:24). In this sense Jesus can be seen as fulfilling the intent of the Mosaic legislation to curb violence. However that fulfillment is accomplished by the complete reversal of the way of retribution embodied in the command. In doing so, the entire system of justice in the Old Testament, which operates on the *lex talionis* principle of retributive justice, is upended, and replaced with the model of restoration and redemption characteristic of the gospel.

Jesus prefaces these above statements by declaring "Do not think that I have come to abolish the Law or the Prophets; I have not come to abolish them but to fulfill them" (Matt 5:17). This is often taken to mean that Jesus is in complete agreement with the law, as if to say "feel free to ignore everything I am about to say." But as we have seen, that is clearly not the case. In fact, one has to ask: why would he feel the need to stress this, unless perhaps he was aware that this was exactly what everyone was thinking. Based on all the things he said and did, it sure looked like he was abolishing the law. But Jesus insists that he is not coming to destroy the law, but to fulfill it. This word in Greek can mean both fulfilling in the sense of *meeting* all the law's requirements, and it can also mean fulfillment in the sense of *perfecting* or *completing* something. Looking at what Jesus then immediately proceeds to do, it becomes abundantly clear that he is referring to this sense of *perfecting* the law, lovingly bringing it into its full intended purpose. In the case of the command to take an "eye for an eye," as we have seen above, that perfecting entailed a complete shift from the system of retributive justice to the system of restorative justice. That is the new law. God's justice is restorative.

3

SALVATION MEANS HEALING

Atonement Rooted in Restorative Justice

PROPONENTS OF PENAL SUBSTITUTION pride themselves in taking sin seriously, and enthusiastically quote Anselm's statement *"you have yet to weigh the gravity of sin."* Yet, penal substitution's legal understanding of individual sin is actually a very superficial one, dealing only with outward behaviors and failing to address the underlying causes rooted in who we are, offering a mere legal acquittal that is powerless to heal us of the true damage sin does to us. In the end, it is penal substitution that has failed to weigh the gravity of sin.

For instance, a bully's maladaptive behavior is an attempt to deal with their underlying insecurity and feelings of worthlessness. It is an attempt to deal with a legitimate need in an inappropriate and hurtful way by devaluing and hurting another in order to make themselves feel powerful. Recognizing this underlying problem (their insecurity) is crucial because one can then address their insecurity—helping them to find better ways to meet that need, and to cope with their negative feelings in a way that does not harm others. A restorative approach, rather than a punitive one, recognizes and addresses our underlying brokenness that leads to hurtful behavior. It is a focus on healing rather than on hurting, on restoration rather than on retribution.

Secondly, an understanding of human brokenness that is solely focused on sin as crime, understood as *hurtful actions done to others*, is inadequate to address the full depth of our need because it is too narrow in scope. It represents of course one important aspect, but the work Christ accomplished entails so much more than this. There are many things that can separate a person from God and life that are about our suffering hurt rather than inflicting it, what is done to us rather than what we do. To name a few examples: people with terminal or debilitating illnesses can often feel abandoned by God, cut off from life and dehumanized. Those who have been victims of abuse can feel dead inside, cut off from love, caught in a destructive cycle of self-loathing. Many people are caught in the cycle of abuse, trapped in dehumanizing poverty, or caught in the perpetual cycles of violence and retaliation around the world—whether they are fought between individuals and tribes, or on the bloody stage of international conflict—leaving orphans, widows, and shattered lives in its wake.

We need an understanding of the gospel that can speak to all of these many ways that people can become estranged from God and life. Self-hatred, abuse, illness, poverty, grief, injustice, and a host of other things can all make a person feel broken, sub-human, and alienated. Our problem is not only the bad things we do, but also the bad things we suffer from others, and from our broken world full of sickness and tragedy. We need to have a model of salvation that can speak to all of these issues, rather than one that is limited to an understanding of our human problem solely focused on transgression.

While this legal tunnel vision has limited the imagination of many theologians, I want to propose that a careful reading of the Gospels shows that Jesus and his understanding of salvation was much broader, and in fact speaks directly to these many needs.

When we look at the ministry of Jesus, we see that the majority of his actions are not focused on calling people to repentance, but rather on ministering to the sick, disabled, and mentally ill, all of which have a direct connection to poverty. In the time of Jesus, illness was seen as God's curse, and as a result people with chronic illness and disability were often ostracized from love and social support. This marginalization understandably led to a spiral of destructive behavior: substance abuse, prostitution, theft, and so on. So we can see that sin (understood as bad behavior) and physical sickness are deeply intertwined.

Once we realize this, the fourfold ministry of Jesus—healing the sick, freeing the demonically oppressed, forgiving the sinner, and caring for the poor—can be seen as addressing the full scope of human brokenness. All of these are part of his salvation work which was not only focused on dealing with moral problems, but dealt with the full person: physically, mentally, spiritually/ethically, and socially.

This fourfold ministry of Jesus all together made up the gospel as Jesus understood and lived it. Each was an integral part of the mission he had come to do. Jesus had not come only to forgive sin, but to liberate us from everything that could separate us from God and life, whether that meant crushing illness, dehumanizing poverty, or spirals of destructive behavior. This is a gospel that addresses us on both an individual and social level, and that takes on the estrangement resulting from suffering and injustice, just as it does the alienation of guilt and shame.

Based on this picture from the Gospels, I would propose that the guiding metaphor we need to adopt in order to understand the depths of our human brokenness and the scope of salvation in Christ is therefore one of sin as *sickness*, rather than sin as *crime*. That is, sin (hurtful behaviors) are merely a symptom of a much larger problem which requires healing rather than punishment.

Now, some may object here that adopting such a "medical model" of sin implies that a person has no moral responsibility. However, this is simply not the case. Certainly, in the Bible moral responsibility is stressed. Likewise, in the fields of both physical and mental illness today, the idea of taking responsibility for one's life is understood as a core part of health and recovery.

The fact that a problem is understood as a "sickness" in no way implies a disavowal of personal responsibility. Some of today's most prominent physical illnesses—heart disease, diabetes, obesity, high blood pressure— are all seen as lifestyle-related. That is, how we live has a direct consequence on our health, and as a result preventive medicine involves making healthy lifestyle choices. Likewise, in the field of mental health, taking responsibility for one's life is considered absolutely crucial to a person's recovery and mental well-being.

So adopting a view of "sin as sickness" does not imply that a person doesn't need to take responsibility for their life. This would reflect a conception of sickness that is out of touch with contemporary understandings in both the fields of mental and physical health. What such a medical paradigm does, however, indicate is that sin is not merely an outward act, but has deep consequences on our being, and that its causes are equally deep-rooted.

Destructive behavior patterns are not simply bad choices one makes in a rational vacuum, they are often linked to past trauma. Consequently, changing those patterns involves working to heal the effects these traumas have had on one's self-image and thinking. In other words, changing the behavior involves addressing the root causes. While this perspective differs from the traditional religious conception of sin understood as a transgression deserving punishment, it is a dynamic that fits very well with what the New Testament describes as the "bondage" of sin.

The medical paradigm adopted by health professionals provides a vastly more sophisticated understanding of the actual dynamics involved in what the Bible calls "sin" than a legal model does. Because of this, it is a model that allows us to address these behaviors much more effectively and deeply than a punitive legal model ever could. Sin—both from the perspective of mental health, and from the New Testament—is a grave illness that requires not simply legal acquittal, but "open heart surgery."

The issue here is not that we restrict ourselves to one particular *metaphor* (note that the language of "bondage" mentioned above evokes the image of slavery rather than sickness), but rather that we have a way of conceptualizing of our human brokenness that leads us to a deep understanding of the underlying issues and complex dynamics involved. I could, for example, speak of someone's "hurtful behavior," using the *language* of healing, but still miss the underlying causes and dynamics behind the outward behavior. The bottom line is that we need a deep understanding, rather than a superficial one. A focus only on outward behavior trivializes the problem.

SIN AS SICKNESS IN THE BIBLE

What I want to really stress at this point is that this deeper understanding of sin as sickness rather than as crime is not in conflict with a biblical understanding. On the contrary, it is *precisely* what the New Testament teaches.

While understanding sin in terms of legal transgression has come to be seen as the "traditional" religious view today, this was not always the case. This legal view of sin was largely formed in the Middle Ages where theology was heavily influenced by the punitive legal thought of the time.

In contrast, the understanding of the early church was much more focused on the idea of sin as sickness and salvation as healing.

For example, Augustine writes in *On Nature and Grace* that "God himself spiritually heals the sick and restores the dead to life, that is, justifies the sinner, through the mediator between God and human beings, the man Jesus Christ . . . God then heals us not only to destroy the sins we have committed, but also to provide us with the means of not sinning."[1] Note here that Augustine makes the ideas of God "healing" and "restoring to life" *synonymous* with justification. Because Augustine's view of human sin was so grave, he does not conceive of it merely as a crime to be remitted, but as a grave wound to be healed: "Relieve a deep wound after Your great healing. Deep is what I have, but in the Almighty I take refuge. Of my own so deadly wound I should despair, unless I could find so great a Physician!"[2]

Why did the early church understand sin and salvation in these medical terms? I would propose that it is because this is the understanding we in fact find in the New Testament as well. As Joel Green declares, "Scripture as a whole presumes the intertwining of salvation and healing" and further, "[t]he larger Roman world of Jesus' day conceived of salvation as healing."[3]

To really grasp this statement we need to dig into the original biblical language a bit: The Greek word that the New Testament uses for *saved* (*sōzō*) can also simultaneously mean *healed*. In fact, Green writes that "the most common usage of these terms in the Greco-Roman world is medical. 'To save' was 'to heal.'"[4]

This verb *sōzō* is frequently used by Jesus in his formulaic phrase "your faith has *saved/healed* you" (Luke 7:50; 8:4; 17:19; 18:42) and it is here that we can see its double meaning at play: When Jesus says to the woman who washes his feet with her tears, "Your sins are forgiven . . . Your faith has saved you" (Luke 7:48, 50), and to the woman with the issue of bleeding who makes her way through the crowd to touch his cloak, "Daughter, your faith has healed you" (Luke 8:48), the phrase in Greek is exactly the same: *hē pistis sou sesōken se*, "your faith has *saved/healed* you." The words are the same, but we translate it as "saved" in one verse and "healed" in the

---

1. Augustine, *On Nature and Grace* 26.29.

2. Augustine, *Exposition on the Psalms*, 51.6. For a study of Augustine's use of the patristic theme of salvation as healing see Arbesmann, "Christus Medicus," 1–28.

3. Green, *Salvation*, 35–36.

4. Ibid., 36.

other based on the context. However, in the original Greek there is a richer interplay going on.

For example, this same phrase is spoken by Jesus to the one leper who returns to give thanks to God (Luke 17:19). Here it is significant that all ten lepers are described as being "healed/restored," (Greek: *iaomai*, v. 15), but only the one who returns is told by Jesus "your faith has saved/healed you." Ten are healed, but only one is *saved-healed* when in response to his healing he turns to God. Consequently, Wolfgang Schrage argues that in these passages *sōzō* is not simply an interchangeable synonym for healing, but entails healing and salvation simultaneously[5]

This double meaning of *sōzō* as salvation/healing is particularly evident in Peter's trial before the Sanhedrin for the healing of a sick man (Acts 4:9–12). When asked by what name or authority he had done this, Peter answers, "this man has been healed (*sōzō*)" in the name of Jesus, and then declares, "There is salvation in no one else; for there is no other name under heaven that has been given among men by which we must be saved (*sōzō*)." Here we have both meanings side by side in the same utterance.

The intertwined meaning of salvation/healing we see here in the New Testament are strengthened when we look at the use of *sōzō* in its larger biblical context. In the LXX *sōzō* usually translates the Hebrew word *yasa* which refers to the deliverance or salvation of Yahweh.[6] As Maureen Yeung argues, these concepts of healing and salvation are inseparable in the Old Testament.[7] Thus while *sōzō* in the LXX denotes *deliverance*, we often find this conceptually tied to healing. Jeremiah cries out in poetic parallel form, "*Heal me* (LXX: *iaomai*), O LORD, and I shall be healed; *save me* (LXX: *sōzō*), and I shall be saved" (Jer 17:14). Likewise, Psalm 107 describes the "redeemed of the Lord" (v. 2) in the same breath as being both "healed" and "delivered from destruction" (v. 20, NRSV). Similarly, healing is often spoken of metaphorically in the sense of our need to be *healed* of sin. David prays, "Have mercy on me, LORD; *heal me*, for I have sinned against you" (Ps 41:4), and of course in Isaiah we read "by his wounds we are *healed*" (Isa 53:5).

Salvation and healing go hand in hand in the Old Testament. God's people are not only *redeemed*, they are also *restored*. This all goes back to

5. Schrage, "Heil und Heilung," 96.

6. The LXX is the Greek translation of the Old Testament used by the authors of the New Testament.

7. Yeung, *Faith in Jesus and Paul*, 53–286.

the fact that in the Old Testament temple ritual healing was understood in terms of cleanliness and uncleanliness. Being healed involved being "made clean," which simultaneously meant being made holy, pure, untainted. So the concepts of healing and sanctification not only go hand in hand, they are virtually synonymous.

With that background in mind, let's jump forward to Jesus, who in framing his understanding of his divine mission and task—declaring why he is here, and what God wants him to be doing—directly connotes sin with sickness: "It is not the healthy who need a doctor, but the sick. I have not come to call the righteous, but sinners to repentance" (Luke 5:31–32; parallels: Matt 9:12–13; Mark 2:17). We have already seen that the ministry of Jesus did not simply address "sinners," but was directed to the sick, the poor, and the oppressed. As Green notes, especially in the Gospel of Luke, the healing ministry of Jesus is not a side note, but rather is the key focus of his salvific work.[8] It is what we see Jesus doing most of the time. It is what salvation looks like. Salvation involves delivering people from both sin and sickness, and these two concepts are often deeply intertwined.[9]

This concept of salvation as *healing* found in the teaching and ministry of Jesus parallels Paul's understanding of justification as *making-righteous* (explored in chapter two and the appendix). For Paul, justification was not merely a legal declaration, rather it entailed *sanctification*. Healing and sanctification thus represent parallel ways of expressing how God acts to *restore* us.

Because our wound is deep (to borrow the phrase from Augustine) we need to understand justification not merely as a legal declaration, but as an inner *transformation* making us healed and holy. Far beyond being simply a kind of legal action, it is a creative act of God that brings life from death.

We can see this illustrated in the story of a paralyzed man who was brought to Jesus. When Jesus said to the man "Take heart, son; your sins are forgiven," the teachers of the law considered this blasphemous. What right did Jesus have to simply declare that his sins were forgiven? Jesus responds to this by saying,

> "Which is easier: to say, 'Your sins are forgiven,' or to say, 'Get up and walk'? But I want you to know that the Son of Man has author-ity on earth to forgive sins." So he said to the paralyzed man, "Get up, take your mat and go home." (Matt 9:5–6).

8. See Green, *The Theology of the Gospel of Luke*, esp. 76–101.
9. See Carroll, "Sickness and Healing in the New Testament Gospels," 130–42.

Jesus here heals the man of his paralysis to demonstrate that when he declares that a person is forgiven he does so with the same authority and transformative power as he does when he heals the sick and lame. The visible reality of the man's healing demonstrates the unseen reality of his forgiveness by God, "*so that you may know* that the Son of Man has authority on earth to forgive sins," Jesus says.

From this we can see that God's forgiveness does not simply mean overlooking an offense; forgiveness entails divine restorative action. As Jesus heals, so does he forgive. His pronouncement of forgiveness is spoken with the same creative authority and power as his pronouncement of physical healing, both resulting in real transformation. The two are inseparable in fact.

HEALING A DEEP WOUND

The irony then, is that it is in fact penal substitution that ends up ignoring sin because it understands salvation as a mere legal acquittal. According to this model, once a substitute is punished in our place, God can then justly overlook our sin. Nothing changes in us, nothing is restored for the one who was hurt. All that happens is that someone is punished, and with that it is declared that the demands of justice have been satisfied. Case closed. This amounts to what many have called a "legal fiction" where the harm our sin does to us and others is simply ignored via a legal loophole.

In contrast, a restorative model recognizes the real harm that sin can do, and seeks to heal it. This involves both caring for those who have been hurt, and restoring those who are hurting others (and if we are honest, we all fall into both of these categories). A restorative model does not deny the problem of sin, but like a doctor, its response is to heal. For example, a doctor may tell a person not to smoke, and warn them that they are putting their lives at risk when they do. However, if that person were later diagnosed with lung cancer the doctor would not refuse treatment. Rather, doctors will do everything in their power to fight the cancer and save the patient's life. That is precisely what God's response to sin is. The gospel is about healing and restoring sinners. It fights the condemnation of the law in the same way that a doctor fights cancer. That is, the way it overcomes the curse is by healing the cancer in us. If the cancer is gone, then the diagnosis is changed. If sin is removed, then condemnation is removed with it. This perspective offers a much deeper way of understanding sin (as sickness rather than crime, thus dealing with the root causes behind the outward symptoms), as well as a more fruitful way of dealing with it (by healing rather than hurting).

4

LOVING SACRIFICE

Understanding Sacrifice as Healing Sanctification

AT THIS POINT YOU might find yourself attracted to a restorative model of salvation and justice. It sounds deeper, saner, and more loving than a punitive view. You are beginning to see that it is also a theme with deep biblical roots as well. You want to believe in it, but find yourself asking "yes, but what about *this* verse . . . ?" One of the goals of this book is to work through as many of those key verses and concepts as possible by showing how they fit into the larger narrative of Scripture, which all culminates in God's redemptive action in Jesus Christ. Restoration is the central plot-line of the New Testament, God's decisive action to bring about justice in Jesus.

Because the legal framework of penal substitution has so saturated our understanding of atonement, there is a tendency to "map" a punitive legal framework onto everything we read in the Bible. When we first begin to see that the New Testament model of salvation is one of restorative justice it can take some time to re-think how we understand concepts like *sacrifice, ransom, being saved, Christ dying for sinners,* and so on in that light. One of the most crucial of these concepts is the idea of sacrifice. Isn't that a legal model? Isn't the sacrifice about appeasing God's anger? Doesn't the book of Hebrews say that there is no forgiveness without the shedding of blood? Isn't Jesus seen as our sacrifice in the New Testament? With those questions in mind, in this chapter we will explore the meaning of the temple sacrifices, seeking to understand them within the context of restorative justice. What I hope to demonstrate is that to understand the temple sacrifice in terms of appeasement is to fundamentally misunderstand it. The sacrifices are correctly understood in terms of healing and sanctification.

TEMPLE SACRIFICE

In attempting to understand the temple sacrifices, it cannot be stressed enough that to think of them in terms of God demanding blood in order to love us is, quite plainly, a grave mischaracterization of what both the theory of penal substitution and the temple sacrifices mean. Sacrifice does not make an angry God loving through appeasement or payment. Even the late John Stott—one of the foremost contemporary proponents of penal substitution—freely admits in *The Cross of Christ*, "[Sacrifice] does not make God gracious . . . God does not love us because Christ died for us, Christ died for us because God loves us."[1] Our repentance is in response to God's love, *not the condition for it.* John Calvin himself—whom many would identify as the founder of the doctrine of penal substitution—makes this same point, quoting from Augustine, "Our being reconciled by the death of Christ must not be understood as if the Son reconciled us, in order that the Father, then hating, might begin to love us."[2] The temple sacrifices are not about appeasement *because God is the initiator.* God does not respond to what we do, we respond to what God does. The sacrifices were a means of atonement provided by a loving God: "I have given it to you to make atonement for yourselves on the altar" (Lev 17:11).

So what was the point of the sacrifices, if it was not to appease? The writers of the Old Testament are emphatic that the main object of sacrifice is not about a mechanical transaction detached from relationship, but the outward ritual effecting inner change, devotion, and repentance. Psalm 51 is traditionally attributed to David's confession of sin. There we read,

---

1. Stott, *Cross of Christ*, 172. At the same time, Stott maintains that the cross is an appeasement of God's wrath. As a result we have the mutually contradictory statement that God does not need to be made gracious . . . but that God must be appeased (which means "made gracious") before God will forgive.

2. Calvin, *Institutes*, II.16.4.

Cleanse me with hyssop, and I will be clean.
Wash me, and I will be whiter than snow . . .
Create in me a pure heart, O God. (Ps 51:7, 10).

David's prayer here is that the outward cleansing of the blood sprinkled from the hyssop branch would go down and cleanse his inmost being. God, David says, is not interested in outward actions, but in the state of his heart.

You do not delight in sacrifice, or I would bring it;
you do not take pleasure in burnt offerings.
My sacrifice, O God, is a broken spirit;
a broken and contrite heart you, God, will not despise.
(Ps 51:16–17).

Echoing this, Isaiah writes that God does not *need* a sacrifice from us. The offering God desires is to see compassion and justice reigning in our lives. God is not interested in detached ritualistic actions or legal requirements, but in a real relational exchange with us that affects us down to the core of our being and flows outwardly into our lives together.

"The multitude of your sacrifices—what are they to me?" says the LORD.
"I have more than enough of burnt offerings,
of rams and the fat of fattened animals;
I have no pleasure in the blood of bulls and lambs and goats . . .
Wash and make yourselves clean. Take your evil deeds out of my sight!
Stop doing wrong, learn to do right! Seek justice: defend the oppressed,
take up the cause of the fatherless, plead the case of the widow."
(Isa 1:11, 16–17).

"I have no pleasure in the blood of bulls and lambs and goats." This statement is crucial for us to hear because of the popular misconception that the saying "without the shedding of blood there is no forgiveness" in Hebrews 9:22 means that God *needs* blood in order to be able to forgive, as if it were some sort of legal requirement. However, reading the entire verse in Hebrews we see it says in full,

The law requires that nearly everything be cleansed with blood,
and without the shedding of blood there is no forgiveness (Heb 9:22).

Here the stated purpose of the blood is not to appease through punishment, but to be "cleansed with blood." Cleansing, or purifying as it is sometimes translated, is associated in this verse with forgiveness. The full formula of Hebrews 9:22 therefore is that without being *cleansed* with blood, there is no forgiveness.

With that in mind, let's return to the passage in Romans that we explored in chapter two. Knowing that the temple sacrifice was about cleaning and purifying, we read the verse "God presented Christ as a sacrifice of atonement" (Rom 3:25) and see that this fits perfectly within the larger context we explored of God's restorative justice making us right. At the same time, it has the function of turning aside God's wrath because if our sin is cleansed, this removes the cause of God's wrath. In technical terms, this means that propitiation comes *through* expiation.[3] That is, wrath is turned away (propitiation) because God cleanses and removes our sin (expiation), thus removing the cause of wrath. We are healed of our sin-sickness, and consequently given a clean bill of health.

This sequence is reversed in penal substitution: There the sacrifice first makes God favorable to us (propitiation) because it satisfies God's anger to have someone punished. Once we are in good standing with God, we can then be cleansed (expiation) because God is now willing to act favorably towards us. However, as we have seen above, virtually every major proponent of penal substitution would agree that the problem is *not* how to make God loving towards us. God has in love provided the means of atonement for us. The problem is the reality of our sin. Remove the sin, and we remove the cause of wrath. Fail to cleanse the sin, and regardless of how much appeasement is made, we cannot be in good standing with God because God cannot be bribed into participating in a legal fiction. Expiation (our cleansing) is the *cause* of propitiation (averting wrath). As the writer of Hebrews tells us, *there is no forgiveness without cleansing.*

A SACRIFICE OF LOVE

Sacrifice is about sanctification. In other words, just as we saw in Romans, forgiveness entails our healing and restoration, our being *made-righteous.* Sin is not a crime that can be acquitted. It is a sickness that requires our being made well again. Recall again David's prayer for forgiveness above "Cleanse me . . . wash me, and I will be whiter than snow . . . Create in me a pure heart, O God" (Ps 51:7, 10). God does not need a sacrifice to forgive us or love us. Rather, we need the sacrifice God provides to be made clean

3. The term "propitiate" means "to make favorable" and is usually associated with the appeasing of anger, while the term "expiate" means "to cleanse" or "remove" the sin itself.

inside. Notice below how the writer of Hebrews continually draws a connection between blood and cleansing, just as in Psalm 51 above:

> The *blood* of goats and bulls and the ashes of a heifer sprinkled on those who are *ceremonially unclean* sanctify them so that they are *outwardly clean.* How much more, then, will the *blood of Christ,* who through the eternal Spirit offered himself unblemished to God, *cleanse* our consciences from acts that lead to death, so that we may serve the living God!" (Heb 9:13–14).

The intent of Christ's sacrifice, we read, is to "purify" (9:23), to "take away sins" (9:28) and "make holy" (10:10; 10:14). There is nothing in Hebrews that indicates that the sacrifices serve to appease wrath through punishment. Throughout Hebrews, sacrifices are described in terms of sanctification and the removal of sin.

That is what the sacrifices mean, but it is crucial to also keep in mind that the temple sacrifice itself is merely a symbol, a metaphor for the real work that Christ has done. The book of Hebrews tells us that the temple sacrifice was a mere "copy and shadow of what is in heaven" (Heb 8:5). The reality is found in Christ who is both the perfect mediator and the perfect sacrifice. The temple sacrifices were an earthly symbol for the heavenly reality realized on the cross. In themselves they were powerless—"Day after day every priest stands and performs his religious duties; again and again he offers the same sacrifices, which can never take away sins" (Heb 10:11)—because they were mere symbols of the reality which was fulfilled in Christ: "For by one sacrifice he has made perfect forever those who are being made holy" (Heb 10:14).

This raises the question: How would the death of Jesus bring about our cleansing? How does Jesus dying make us holy? Especially intriguing here is that Hebrews speaks of Christ's death in terms of a "sacrifice" and at the same time disavows ritual sacrifice. Quoting from Psalm 40, "Sacrifices and offerings, burnt offerings and sin offerings you did not desire, nor were you pleased with them" the author of Hebrews concludes that the ritual of sacrifice has been abandoned in place of Jesus doing God's will, "And by that will, we have been made holy through the sacrifice of the body of Jesus Christ once for all" (Heb 10:10). In other words, it is not the death of Jesus in itself, but rather *the obedience of Jesus*—his faithfulness to love—that acts to make us holy.

It is love that led Jesus to the cross. Love is the focus, not death. This entails a major shift in how sacrifice is understood from the old covenant to the new: Whereas temple sacrifice was a legal requirement, the sacrifice of Jesus is understood here in terms of doing God's will by acting in love. Jesus tells his disciples that there is no greater love conceivable than for someone to give their life for their friends (John 15:3). Paul amplifies this by saying that God loved us in this way "while we were still sinners," while we were "God's enemies" (Rom 5:8–10). So when we think of Jesus as a "sacrifice" the New Testament emphasis is on his act of loving which Jesus exhibited throughout his entire life. Paul consequently encourages us to become "living sacrifices" by caring for one another and exhibiting enemy love (Rom 12:1–21). This is typified by Jesus' quotation from the prophet Hosea: "I desire mercy, not sacrifice." The focus here is on prioritizing care for people over ritual observance (Matt 9:13; 12:7).

Here a distinction René Girard makes between the ritual of sacrifice and the sacrifice of Christ is helpful. When an interviewer described Girard as advocating a "non-sacrificial" reading of the death of Christ, he responded, "It is not quite true that I take what you have called a 'non-sacrificial reading of the death of Christ.' We must establish first of all that there are two kinds of sacrifice."[4] To those familiar with Girard's work, this may seem like somewhat of an about-face, or at least a modification of his former position, since in *Things Hidden Since the Foundation of the World* he explicitly states that his aim is to propose a "non-sacrificial reading" of the death of Christ.[5] In response to the interviewer, however, Girard distinguishes between two models of sacrifice. He illustrates the two with the story from 1 Kings 3 where two women claim to be the mother of an infant, and Solomon offers to cut a baby in half.

> When Solomon offers to split the child, the one woman says "Yes" because she wishes to triumph over her rival. The other woman then says, "No, she may have the child," because she seeks only its life. On the basis of this love, the king declares that "she is the mother." . . . The first woman is willing to sacrifice a child to the needs of rivalry. Sacrifice is the solution to mimetic rivalry and the foundation of it. The second woman is willing to sacrifice everything she wants for the sake of the child's life. This is sacrifice in the sense of the gospel. It is in this sense that Christ is a sacrifice since he gave himself "for the life of the world."[6]

4. Girard, "An Interview with René Girard."

5. Girard, *Things Hidden*, 187.

6. Girard, "An Interview with René Girard."

Hebrews similarly points to the true meaning of "sacrifice" as focused on Christ's "doing God's will" through self-giving love exemplified throughout the entire life and ministry of Jesus. This New Testament understanding of sacrifice reflects the way we commonly use the term today. As a parent, I might for example speak of the many "sacrifices" I make for my children. Sacrifice here means giving something at great cost out of love. We see this same understanding of sacrifice defined as costly love exhibited throughout the New Testament.[7]

As with the rest of the New Testament, Hebrews therefore speaks both of the *fulfillment* of sacrifice in Christ, and at the same time the *end of sacrifice*. In other words, the meaning of the sacrifice is changed from a ritual requirement to an act of love that brings our healing. Secondly, God does not receive a sacrifice, but *becomes it*. Instead of us reaching up to God, God reached down to us. It is not we who act to make things right, but God who acts. It is God in Christ who both *provides* and *is* the sacrifice. God in Christ *becomes the sacrifice* through the cross. So even if any of the Gentile converts in the early days of the church were to understand the sacrifice of Christ based on their own pagan understandings of appeasing or placating the anger of the gods, that idea of appeasement is turned on its head since you can no more appease or bribe yourself than you can steal from yourself. This reversal of the sacrifice is in keeping with the many reversals that Jesus taught—the greatest is the servant, blessed are the least, die to live, and so on. What we have therefore is a focus on love leading to healing, and at the same time (as Girard notes) a critique of the injustice of scapegoating. Both of these will be explored in more detail in later chapters.

Now this all still leaves us with several unanswered questions: If it was not the nails, but love that held Jesus to the cross, then how exactly does that self-sacrificing love make us holy? How is this connected to Christ's death "for us"? These are themes that we will explore at length as the book progresses. But we need to first understand the *meaning* before we can get to the mechanics. We need to understand *what* the sacrifice means before we address *how* it works. If we wish to understand sacrifice as the New Testament does, our starting point is to think of it in the context of healing and restoration, and as a demonstration of costly love.

7. For example John 15:13; Rom 8:32; 12:1; Gal 1:4; 2:20; Eph 5:2; 5:25; Phil 2:17; 4:18, Titus 2:14.

5

CHRISTUS VICTOR

The Drama of Restorative Justice

In previous chapters we explored a restorative model of salvation rooted in the concept of healing the sickness of sin. As we saw, this is a perspective that is not only found in the New Testament, but is also reflective of the church fathers' understanding of salvation as healing. That restorative model is known as Christus Victor.

The term "Christus Victor" comes from the title of a book written in 1931 by Gustav Aulén.[1] The book is a historical study of atonement theories throughout the history of the church from its inception up to the early twentieth century. Based on his study of the early church fathers, Aulén contrasts what he identifies as the "classic" and "Latin" views of the atonement, showing how the "classic" view (i.e., Christus Victor) was predominant for the first 1000 years of the church's history, until it was gradually replaced by the "Latin" view of the cross as exemplified by Anselm in his theory of legal "satisfaction."[2]

1. Aulén, *Christus Victor*.

2. In addition to Aulén's work, see also my article in *Evangelical Quarterly* where I identify the themes of *healing* and *liberation* in the context of restorative justice throughout the writings of the Church Fathers (Flood, "Substitutionary atonement and the Church Fathers"). When Christus Victor is understood in terms of these dual themes of healing and liberation (as I believe Aulén intends), this can indeed be identified as the "classic" patristic view, in contrast to the later "Latin" view based on retributive justice.

Christus Victor is a picture of God in Christ liberating humanity out of bondage from sin, death, and the devil. Thus we could say that the "classic" view is characterized by a central theme of *liberation* in the context of *restorative* justice, whereas the later "Latin" view is characterized by a central theme of *appeasement* in the context of *retributive* justice. Walter Wink explains the reasons for this major shift:

> The Christus Victor theology fell out of favor, not because of intrinsic inadequacies, but because it was subversive to the church's role as a state religion. The church no longer saw the demonic as lodged in the empire, but in the empire's enemies. Atonement became a highly individualized transaction between the believer and God; society was assumed to be Christian, so the idea that the work of Christ entails the radical critique of society was largely abandoned.[3]

In other words, there was a shift from an understanding of the atonement understood in the context of *restorative justice* and entailing a critique of empire (Christus Victor) to one rooted in *punitive justice* which therefore supported empire (satisfaction/penal substitution). The chart below diagrams these two models and how we can perceive the same information differently depending on which lens we view it through.

Two Models:	Punitive	Restorative
Why was the Messiah sinless?	To present a perfect offering	To model the values of the Kingdom
Why did the Messiah have to suffer?	To *appease* authority	To *liberate* from false authority
Where is the culmination of the messianic work?	Focus on *cross* where penalty was paid	Focus on *resurrection* where sin and death were overcome

In the Latin *punitive model* the reason the Messiah came was to pay a penalty. In the *restorative model* the reason the Messiah came was to liberate and restore. In the *punitive model* the reason the Messiah needed to be sinless is to present a perfect offering. In the *restorative model* the reason the Messiah needed to be sinless is to present a model of God's heart (Christ's nature) and values (Christ's Kingdom). In the *punitive model* the reason the Messiah had to suffer is to appease authority. In the *restorative*

---

3. Wink, *Engaging the Powers*, 150. See also Weaver "Atonement for the Non-Constantinian Church," 307–23.

model the reason the Messiah had to suffer is to free us from the grip of false authority—to liberate us from sin, death, and the devil.

If we want to understand what the biblical writers meant by the concepts of *salvation, deliverance, ransom, redemption,* and *messiah,* we need to understand their worldview and way of thinking, rather than projecting the worldview of the Middle Ages (or our contemporary one, for that matter) onto what they were saying. Aulén has traced this theme within the writings of the early church, but its roots go further back than this. As we will see in the following section, the themes of liberation and healing found in Christus Victor not only find their roots in Scripture, they represent the central metanarrative of the Old Testament which shaped the Jewish people's understanding of salvation, stretching from Moses to Malachi to the Messiah.

SCRIPTURE'S MESSIANIC METANARRATIVE

The biblical roots of Christus Victor are found in the Old Testament's story of the exodus out of slavery in Egypt. The exodus was the story through which the Jews understood who they were, who God was, and made sense of their world: They were a people who belonged to a God who had miraculously led them into freedom. Their hope was that God would again bring them out of exile and into the reign of God, bringing with it justice and restoration.

The exodus is the central defining narrative of the Old Testament that everything else draws from, "not only as historic event," Joel Green writes, "but also as the lens through which to make sense of present experience and as the matrix within which to shape future hopes."[4] We can see this as the psalmists and Prophets cry out to God for justice and liberation. In his distress, the psalmist is constantly recalling how God, in days of old, redeemed the Israelites out of slavery in the land of Egypt, "I will remember the deeds of the LORD; yes, I will remember your miracles of long ago . . . With your mighty arm you redeemed your people" (Ps 77:11, 15). Likewise, throughout the prophets, a people now in exile are reminded of the time where the Lord had redeemed them out of slavery: "I brought you up out of Egypt, and redeemed you from the land of slavery" (Mic 6:4).

This remembrance of the exodus was the foundation of the hope of deliverance and redemption out of exile.

4. Green, *Salvation*, 66.

> "However, the days are coming," declares the LORD, "when it will no longer be said, 'As surely as the LORD lives, who brought the Israelites up out of Egypt,' but it will be said, 'As surely as the LORD lives, who brought the Israelites up out of the land of the north and out of all the countries where he had banished them.' For I will restore them to the land I gave their ancestors." (Jer 16:14–15)

And again,

> For the LORD will deliver Jacob and redeem them from the hand of those stronger than they . . . This is what the LORD Almighty, the God of Israel, says: "When I bring them back from captivity . . . "The days are coming," declares the LORD, "when I will make a new covenant with the people of Israel and with the people of Judah. It will not be like the covenant I made with their ancestors when I took them by the hand to lead them out of Egypt, . . . I will put my law in their minds and write it on their hearts. I will be their God, and they will be my people." (Jer 31:11–33, and cf. Heb 10:15–17)

Walter Bruggemann states that "Israel characteristically retold *all* of its experience through the powerful, definitional lens of the exodus memory."[5] N.T. Wright similarly states that "it is hard to overestimate the importance of the exodus story within the historical, political, and theological worldview of Second Temple Judaism."[6] Consequently, the language of *salvation*, *redemption*, and *ransom*, found throughout the biblical narrative, all have deep roots pointing back to the central defining event of the exodus out of slavery, and forward to the hope of deliverance from oppression and the restoration of God's rule. So when Jesus speaks of his life being a "ransom," this does not merely refer generically to purchasing a slave's freedom, but would have almost certainly been immediately understood in the Jewish context of God ransoming Israel from bondage in the exodus. Paul's term "redemption" likewise would recall the exodus story of Israel's redemption from slavery. Even when the New Testament speaks of "payment" in reference to our salvation, this is always framed in the context of being ransomed out of slavery and bondage: "You were bought at a price; do not become slaves of human beings" (1 Cor 7:23).

The self-identity of the Jewish people throughout the entire Old Testament was one of a people longing to break free from oppression, of a people

---

5. Bruggemann, *Theology of the Old Testament*, 177. Emphasis in original.

6. Wright, *Jesus and the Victory of God*, 577.

crying out for justice—for things to be made right. Today we too live in a world filled with suffering and injustice, with broken lives and abusive relationships. We are bombarded on the nightly news with images of war, starvation, and terror until we too cry out like the psalmist, "How long, Lord? How long?" This cry for justice and liberation is the central theme of the prophets and the ground from which the messianic hope sprang. The Messiah would be the one to come and set things right, restoring justice, liberating the people from bondage and oppression, and establishing God's reign. That is what the messianic hope is about: not merely a change in politics or individual fate, but for God's loving justice to rule both inside and out, for the whole world to be made well again.[7]

THE NEW EXODUS

Into that context of a people shaped by the hopes of the exodus narrative comes Jesus, preaching the message of God's kingdom, healing the sick, and forgiving sins, casting out demons, and proclaiming good news to the poor and oppressed. His focus is on ministering to the sinner, the unclean, the demonically oppressed, and the poor—to people who had been "exiled" to the margins of society. For such people, these are not simply literary themes; they speak to their very real experience of bondage, and to their deepest longings for restoration and release. In the Gospel of Luke, Jesus inaugurates his ministry by directly connecting his work with the promise of the liberation of God's people out of exile, prophesied by Isaiah:

> The Spirit of the Lord is on me,
> because he has anointed me to proclaim good news to the poor.
> He has sent me to proclaim freedom for the prisoners
> and recovery of sight for the blind, to set the oppressed free,
> to proclaim the year of the Lord's favor.
> (Luke 4:18–19, quoting Isa 61:1–2)

Jesus frames his messianic task here in the terms of liberating those in captivity, healing the blind, and releasing those in prison—all of which are classic Christus Victor themes. The central metaphors with which he chose to describe his own death were *ransom* (which as we have seen recalls the exodus and liberation from bondage) and the *Passover* (which likewise recalls the exodus). At the last supper, Jesus reappropriates the bread and

---

7. See Wright, *The New Testament and the People of God*, 157–61.

wine of Passover and applies them to himself. Taking up the "cup of redemption," (remember the word "redemption" means being set free from bondage) he tells his disciples this cup now represents a new covenant in his blood, asking his disciples to now associate the memory of exodus with him whenever they celebrate the Passover: "Do this, whenever you drink it, in remembrance of me" (1 Cor 11:25, where Paul cites the Jesus tradition).

This "New Passover" effected by Jesus, while having a direct parallel to the Old Testament's exodus metanarrative, is at the same time significantly different: While the enemies in the exodus story were other people (the Egyptians), the "enemy" in the gospel is evil itself. Moreover, in Jesus all of humanity is the recipient of God's deliverance, rather than one particular ethnic group, as in the exodus. Christ's death is therefore analogous to Passover and at the same time, in these significant ways, quite different from it. Jesus re-enacts the history of Israel, but in a way that is truly a new covenant, and a new exodus.

Perhaps the most significant shift is the notion of a crucified messiah. Many, if not most first-century Jews expected the messiah to be a man of war, and for the liberation to come through violent force. We see this reflected in the disciples' own expectations for Jesus. Jesus, however, did not come to take life, but to give his own life. The gospel is indeed about the messiah's "victory" over evil and injustice, but that messianic victory does not come through violent conquest and military force, but through restoration and healing. In the New Testament a shift has taken place where this same vocabulary of liberation is now used to speak, not of overcoming enemy nations, but of overcoming *the* Enemy—in us and in our world. Ephesians states that our struggle is not directed against "flesh and blood" humans, but against evil itself, manifest in "the powers of this dark world, and against the spiritual forces of evil in the heavenly realms" (Eph 6:12).

As much as it is important to understand the continuity between the Old and New Testament in the context of the exodus narrative, it is equally important to note the radical discontinuity. God's ultimate victory and the defeat of evil in Christ does not come through power and violence, but rather through the weakness of the cross. Likewise, the way of the cross— the way of enemy love—becomes the new rule that governs our lives and world. Christus Victor (that is, the new exodus) is a dramatic narrative of humanity's liberation from evil that provides the *conceptual framework* within which we can understand the atonement. This conceptual framework is one of *nonviolent restorative justice.*[8]

CHRISTUS VICTOR AS THEO-DRAMA

Scripture is written primarily as narrative. The Gospels, for instance, are all written in narrative form—as stories. As a result, rather than having a simple formula for how salvation works, we see it lived out in the life and ministry of Jesus. As Jesus encounters people in their need we see that he does not have one pat way of dealing with people. Each person Jesus encounters differently. He tells one person to "go home" (Matt 9:6), when in the chapter before he tells another *not* to go home (Matt 8:22). Sometimes he forgives, sometimes he confronts. As a result, the narrative form of the Gospels gives us a very complex picture. Like other narrative forms, such as a novel or a film, it contains many interweaving, and even seemingly contradictory, themes that together shape the larger story. These narrative forms reflect the complexity of our real lives in a way that formulas never could.

All too often, the ministry and teaching of Jesus have been seen by proponents of penal substitution as something to fast-forward through so we can get to the cross. But as Martin Kähler famously said, the Gospels are in fact "passion narratives with an extended introduction."[9] The Gospels' record of the ministry and teaching of Jesus therefore represent the best commentary and insight we have available to us into how Christ understood his messianic work. It is in this context of the whole life and way of Christ, and only in this context, that we can understand his cross.

Consequently, one of the central points that Aulén makes is that Christus Victor should not be understood as a formula describing the mechanics of the atonement, but rather as the narrative of God's grace breaking into our lives, expressed in the dramatic terms of a struggle between God and the devil, or as Luther puts it, between the "tyrant of sin" and the "righteousness of Christ." In this sense, Christus Victor is not a *theory* of the atonement at all (in the sense of a doctrinal formula), it is a *narrative theme* expressed in many different ways.

---

8. This focus on nonviolence is perhaps the most important insight of Mennonite theologian J. Denny Weaver's articulation of Christus Victor in his book *The Nonviolent Atonement.*

9. Kähler, *The So-Called Historical Jesus*, 80 n. 11.

These themes of liberation from oppression, restoration, and healing are not simply isolated motifs found in individual verses. They represent a broad narrative trajectory of how salvation was understood. That narrative is begun in the meta-narrative of the exodus, and takes on new form as it is picked up in the narratives of the Gospels where the messiah has come to bring healing and restoration to humanity, defeat evil, and establish God's kingdom rule.

Once we have identified this narrative in the Gospels, it is easy to see it echoed throughout the rest of the New Testament. John sums up the entire work of Christ, saying, "The reason the Son of God appeared was to destroy the devil's work" (1 John 3:8). Hebrews similarly states that the purpose of Christ's death was that "he might break the power of him who holds the power of death—that is, the devil" (Heb 2:14). Colossians describes this in terms of our liberation into a new identity, "For he has rescued us from the dominion of darkness and brought us into the kingdom of the Son he loves" (Col 1:13).

In understanding Christus Victor as a *narrative*, we must differentiate it from what is known as the "ransom theory" of the atonement. The key factor here is that ransom theory is focused on the *mechanics* of the atonement, describing in legal terms how God ransomed humanity (that is, *purchased* us out of slavery) from the devil. It is a legal *formula*, rather than a narrative theme. Thus the discussion revolves around legal questions of *who* the payment was to (God or the devil), whether the devil *deserved* any payment, and so on.

Of course what this all misses is the original Jewish context of ransom: God did not "pay" Pharaoh when ransoming Israel from bondage. Ransom understood in the context of the exodus narrative is not about payment; it is about liberation. Ransom theory has removed these themes of liberation from their narrative context in the new exodus, and reduced it to a legal formula. It was the ransom theory of the atonement framed as a rational legal formula that Anselm (and later Ritschl) rejected. Today many theologians likewise regard ransom theory as "crude," and indeed it is.

The problem is that Anselm, and those who followed his example, simply replaced it with another rational legal formula (Anselm's satisfaction theory, and then later the Reformer's penal substitution theory) which also trivialized the problem of sin. In fact, *all* atonement theories, when understood in rationalistic legal terms, become shallow and crude. This is equally true for penal substitution *and* Christus Victor. What matters is getting hold of the *meaning*, not the mechanics, and we do this by getting behind the *drama* of these powerful metaphors which describe the complex dynamics of sin, and the narrative of God's act of liberating humanity from it.

Christus Victor should therefore not be understood as a *theory* of the atonement at all—if by a theory one means a formula with which to explain the reason(s) for the atonement. Rather, it is a collection of dramatic motifs and narrative images that give insight into the dynamics of sin and evil, and the narrative of God's struggle to redeem humanity from their grip. Its focus is on the *meaning*, the big picture, the contextual narrative framework of the atonement. It is atonement understood as a narrative of restoration, rather than as a legal exchange formula.[10]

Unfortunately, this is something that many systematic theologians do not seem to grasp, focusing on the dramatic language, but seeming to miss the larger narrative framework it points to. Roger Olson sums up a typical complaint,

> "It is too dramatic, too poetic to provide a rational answer to the question [of why Christ had to die]. That is not to dismiss the Christus Victor concept . . . It is great sermonic material! However, alone it cannot satisfy inquiring minds who want theologically meaningful constructive models that answer the why question."[11]

Now, I am very sympathetic to Olson and his desire to ask these "why" questions of the cross. Addressing these questions (why did Jesus need to die? How does the cross save/heal us? etc.) will be the focus of chapter 9. However, as someone who has worked for more than two decades as a professional artist and filmmaker, I also have to respectfully say that such complaints seem to reveal a lack of appreciation for the depth and insight that we can gain through story. Properly understood, drama is not simply about emotionalism and histrionics: It is the central structure we humans use for making sense of our complex lives. In other words, before we can get to the specific "why" questions of the mechanics of the atonement, we first need to understand the big picture that Christus Victor provides. Specifically, that narrative is one of the triumph of God's way of nonviolent restoration in Christ over fallen religion's way of violent retribution. Without that narrative framework to anchor our understanding of what salvation is about,

---

10. Thus the *narrative* of ransom (that is, the theme of liberation from bondage exemplifiedin the exodus story and portrayed in the Gospel narratives) is reflective of Christus Victor, while ransom *theory* is not.

11. Olson, *The Mosaic of Christian Beliefs*, 259.

we will read the supporting metaphors out of context and thus get all of the "why" questions wrong.

Furthermore, the language of narrative is dramatic precisely because it addresses things that matter. We cannot truly understand something when we observe it "objectively" from a distance. We understand when it pounds in our chest, when it *impacts* us. We only truly know something when we are in the middle of it. These are vital matters of life and death that cannot be captured in a simplified formula, but must be articulated narratively and poetically as living ideas that move and touch us at the core of who we are. Spiritual things must be spoken of in the language of analogy and drama because they are so much beyond our words to capture, and because we need the passion that these images evoke to get hold of the depth and gravity of these ideas.

6

THE TYRANT OF WRATH

Unmasking the Bondage of Personal and Systemic Evil

IN THE PREVIOUS CHAPTER we looked at Christus Victor's dramatic narrative of salvation, tracing it through both the Old and New Testaments. In this chapter we turn to explore how that narrative plays out in the drama of our own lives. A major element of the narrative drama of Christus Victor is the New Testament's language of the devil and demons. In the beginning of the twentieth century, many modernist liberal theologians stumbled over what sounded to them like superstition, and as a result rejected Christus Victor. That has largely changed today due to an increased appreciation of metaphor.

The key, as Aulén argued, is getting behind what may seem to us as odd mythological vocabulary and focusing on the *reality* it points to. "It should be evident," Aulén writes, "that the historical study of dogma is wasting its time in pure superficiality if it does not endeavor to penetrate to that which lies below the outward dress and look for the religious values which lie concealed underneath."[1]

Thankfully, since Aulén wrote those words back in 1931, there has been a growing appreciation that the dramatic struggle described by the Christus Victor view address very real things—the reality of radical evil, the debilitating effects of oppression on the human heart, abusive authority's

1. Aulén, 47.

crippling impact on our self-image, and structural evil which holds people in cycles of poverty, racism, abuse, and injustice. Understanding these dynamics—the complex reality that the dramatic imagery of Christus Victor points to—will be the focus of this chapter.

FALLEN AUTHORITY

As we saw in chapter 3, viewing our human brokenness in terms of sickness in need of healing provides much deeper insights into the dynamics involved than a model of "sin as crime" does. That is why this model has been widely adopted today, and we think in terms of mental *health*. The way we conceptualize an issue affects what we are able to see. Viewing human brokenness simply in terms of transgression (sin as crime) leads us to a very superficial understanding of what is really going on, and thus what the solution is.

A major theme of Christus Victor is how systems of authority can become fallen and sinful, just as individuals can. Good things (such as family, religion, and law) can all become abusive, corrupted, and profoundly hurtful. Within traditional Reformed theology, because it conceptualizes of sin in terms of moral transgression (sin as crime), this concept is virtually unknown. Instead, sin is conceptualized solely in terms of our individual transgression. We transgress *from* the authority. The authority itself (the family, the church, the law) is seen as the one who accuses, but never as the potential source of the problem.

This major blind-spot can have devastating consequences for our own self-understanding, as well as for our image of God. Take for example the following passage from J. I. Packer, who addresses the very real problem of a person haunted by the guilt of their past,

> When Lady Macbeth, walking and talking in her sleep, sees blood on her hand, and cannot clean or sweeten it, she witnesses to the order of retribution as all writers of tragedy and surely all reflective men—certainly, those who believe in penal substitution—have come to know it: wrongdoing may be forgotten for a time . . . but sooner or later it comes back to mind . . . and at once our attention is absorbed, our peace and pleasure are gone, and *something tells us that we ought to suffer for what we have done.* When joined with inklings of God's displeasure, *this sense of things is the start of hell.* Now it is into this context of awareness that the model of penal substitution is introduced . . . Insight one concerns God; it is that

> the retributive principle has his sanction, and indeed expresses the
> holiness, justice and goodness reflected in his law.[2]

Now if our sense of guilt means taking moral responsibility for our lives (evidenced in feelings of remorse and leading to repentance and restitution), this would of course be a good thing. However, these same feelings of guilt—in Packer's words, the idea that "we ought to suffer for what we have done"—can also lead people into the self-hatred of addiction, destructive behavior, and even suicide. Packer is quite right to call this "the beginning of Hell," but we must seriously question whether that spiral into self-focused destruction indeed has the "sanction of God," as he claims.

The feeling that we "ought to suffer," mentioned by Packer, points to internalized shame which mental health professionals say is often linked to the experience of emotional and physical abuse.[3] In her groundbreaking book, Patricia Evans lists the following among the "primary consequences of verbal abuse" for its victims: "An inclination to soul searching and re-viewing incidents with the hope of determining what went wrong, a loss of self-confidence, a growing self-doubt," and "an internalized 'critical voice.'"[4] What this means is that when a person who has been the victim of abuse does not face this in themselves and enters into a faith community which encourages such self-loathing and internalized shame, telling them that these feelings in fact have God's "sanction," this effectively aligns God's will with that of their abuser.

In drawing attention to this, it is not my intent to point fingers or place blame, but I do wish to raise awareness and sensitivity to the fact that such teaching and theology can potentially do considerable damage to people's self-image as well as to their image of God. This death trap of guilt is not what God desires; it is what Christ has come to save us *from*. These false gods of Condemnation, Guilt, Legalism, Self-Hatred, and Abuse are the unmerciful judges who will not let go of their hold on us. The Accuser, the Father of Lies, the Condemner, is the one who demands satisfaction. To the extent that we have internalized the "god of this world" (2 Cor 4:4, NRSV), our own internal critic is the one who will not forgive us, who constantly speaks condemnation in our ear: *"How could God love someone as sinful as*

---

2. Packer, "Logic of Penal Substitution" 29–30. Emphasis added.

3. Lenore Walker has written extensively on this topic, and her research has been pivotal in the mental health field today. For an introduction, see Walker, *The Battered Woman Syndrome*.

4. Evans, *The Verbally Abusive Relationship*, 48.

you!?" Through internalizing this inner judge, a person in an abusive and dehumanizing situation actually comes to see themselves as *deserving* of abuse and condemnation. *"You are worthless trash. This all your fault,"* our inner judges cry out.

This is not only the case for victims of abuse, but can be equally true for criminals as well, who—through their own destructive, cruel, and selfish behavior—have sown the seeds of their own destruction, and find themselves consequently hated and condemned by others. Once they can begin to face what they have done, they too hear the voice of condemnation and judgment, the Accuser, who whispers: *"You can never change; you're rotten down to core. Why fight it?"* Both the victim and the criminal here are equally prisoners to Sin and Death. Whether through their own hurtfulness or through the hurtfulness of others, both are now trapped in Hell's vicious circle of sowing and reaping, of hurting and being hurt.

Our problem is not simply our hurtful actions, but how shame and guilt can become tyrants, enslaving us in a world of alienation, fear, and self-hatred. I have purposely chosen Packer to illustrate this—not because he represents the worst of penal substitution, but because he represents the theory at its very best. Packer is a brilliant theologian with a great heart for the lost, who in the above passage was attempting to show through a dramatic presentation of penal substitution how it addresses the needs of those plagued with guilt. The problem with Packer's view (which is typical of conservative Reformed theology in general) is that the New Testament concepts of fallenness, bondage, and the satanic are all left out of his understanding of sin. The sole players are reduced to man and God, and sin is conceptualized solely in terms of individual transgression. As a result, he is compelled to conclude that feelings of self-loathing must be God's will.

In so doing, such theologians unwittingly end up giving divine sanction to self-hatred and abuse. Instead of recognizing this as something that is horribly broken which leads to death, it is set it up as the ultimate expression of God's "holiness, justice, and goodness." Because these theologians quite literally place God in the biblical role of Satan, the Accuser, their portrayal of God is understandably perceived by many as abusive.

This painfully illustrates that it is not only we who are fallen. At times it is our theology—our very conception of authority and justice—that is fallen as well. Christ has come to redeem us *from* the curse of the retributive principle. God has come in Christ to ransom us from Satan's dominion, not to affirm it.

A FALLEN WORLD

With these dynamics in mind, let's take a closer look at what scripture tells us about fallenness and the nature of evil. In Christian thought, Satan is not an independently evil being, as in dualism, but a fallen angel. Evil thus involves the picture of a good thing that has fallen from its original purpose and has become twisted and warped. The more potential something has for good, the more harm it can cause if it turns bad. Families, for instance, are meant to be safe and loving environments where we learn to love ourselves and others, but when twisted by sin, families can be profoundly damaging and abusive, leaving lifelong scars. The very things that have enslaved us were originally good things that have become warped and twisted. Precisely because they began as good things, we trust their authority in our lives, and are taken captive by them. Conscience can turn to condemnation, scruple twists itself into repression, morality becomes legalism.

Paul tells us how the law—a good thing that was intended to bring life—actually brought him death and condemnation. Instead of pointing him to God it became an end in itself, a replacement for God. Paul speaks of how he had been "sold as a slave to sin" by the law (Rom 7:14), but by grace he has been "set free" (Rom 8:2). Does this mean that the Law is itself bad, Paul asks? No. Paul explains that sin had twisted the law into something it was never meant to be, so that it had become "death" to him (cf. Rom 7:7–14).

For this reason Christus Victor speaks not only of our liberation from these "tyrants" (as Luther calls them), but of their being overcome by Christ. Paul tells us that because of the resurrection, Christ will destroy "all dominion, authority, and power," and put them under his feet (1 Cor 15:24–25). In other words, we are not only liberated from the abusive system, that fallen system itself is put under Christ as well.

Picking up on this theme, church fathers such as Athanasius and Gregory of Nazianzus speak of death and curse being "abolished" and "annulled" by Christ.[5] Augustine declares that, as a result of the atonement, "death was condemned that its reign might cease, and cursed that it might be destroyed."[6] Not only do we die to sin, but the law of condemnation itself,

---

5. Athanasius writes that because of the Christ's death, "death and corruption were in the same act utterly abolished." (Athanasius, *On the Incarnation*, 2). Gregory similarly declares that Christ "destroyed the whole condemnation of your sins" (Gregory of Nazianzus, *Oration* 40, 45).

6. Augustine, *Contra Faustum*, 14.3.

the retributive principle, is condemned and crucified: "Erasing the record that stood against us with its legal demands. He set this aside, nailing it to the cross" (Col 2:14, NRSV). Paul then declares in the following verse that through the cross, abusive authority is exposed and disarmed: "And having disarmed the powers and authorities, he made a public spectacle of them, triumphing over them by the cross" (Col 2:15).

Now we need to be careful with this "victory motif" in Christus Victor so as not to take it simply in triumphalist terms contrary to the entire message and example of Jesus. The full picture of what Paul understands this "triumph" to mean is that law, religion, conscience—and a host of other *good* things that have become fallen and hurtful to us—should not simply be rejected and thrown away. Rather, like us, they are in need of being reformed and redeemed. Grace redeems both us and the very laws that condemned us, placing all under Christ. Our broken images of family, morality, and authority are redeemed out of their hurtful and dominating position, and put under the higher law of grace (cf. Rom 8:1–17). Christ's death was not only for us, but involved the redemption of law and authority as well. We are redeemed, and so are the laws and systems and rules.

How does this redemption of the law of retribution look? Paul writes that "we have been released from the law so that we serve in the new way of the Spirit" (Rom 7:6). That is, the way of grace and restoration supersedes the way of law and retribution, and thus fulfills what it could not. "Therefore," Paul concludes, "love is the fulfillment of the law" (Rom 13:10).

Here we must keep two things in tension: First, while the New Testament does offer a severe critique of religion and authority itself, we must understand this judgment within the larger trajectory of redemption. To speak of the law only as "abolished" and "destroyed" does not take into account the larger purpose of restorative justice, which ultimately seeks to restore these systems to serve their proper role under Christ. Second, at the same time—especially because of the church's history of collusion with abusive power—we dare not whitewash over the New Testament's very real critique of the abuse of religious authority exemplified in Jesus' confrontation with the Pharisees, and in Paul's critique of the law which the early church picked up on in language of "abolishing" the powers. Just as we need to be self-aware and introspective, we also need to be aware of how authority can become fallen. As history shows, the church has not been particularly good at this, often defending the status quo rather than those on the margins.

STRUCTURAL EVIL

So far in this chapter, our focus has been on exploring how fallen authority affects us as individuals. In the terms of Christus Victor: we are liberated out of hurtful authority and restored into a healthy and loving relationship with God. The focus here is on our redemption as individuals. This is of course crucial, but the scope of salvation is much larger than this, entailing not only our redemption, but the redemption of our fallen institutions, societies, churches, families, and communities as well. In other words, we see in the broad perspective of the Christus Victor narrative that the work of Christ addresses corporate and structural sin as well as individual sin—the transformation of individuals, and the transformation of our world.

Conservative evangelicals tend to believe that if individuals repent, the system will automatically change.[7] But changed lives do not automatically change structural problems. Think for instance about a sweatshop: Even if many individual managers in the sweatshop become compassionate people, this alone will not change that system, which forces children to work grueling hours in unsafe conditions. There needs to be structural reform, as well, which affects the system itself. Changed individuals need to work to change their world. The Lordship of Christ needs to be applied to the larger evils of poverty, racism, starvation, violence, and corporate greed on a *structural* level.

The New Testament has quite a bit to say about the evil of structures and systems, and how they are impacted by the work of Christ. It expresses this in terms of "kingdoms" and "powers." Paul for instance begins his letter to the Colossians by accounting how they were "rescued from the *dominion* of darkness" and brought "into the *kingdom* of the Son" (Col 1:13). This of course involves our personal reconciliation with God, but Paul broadens this to include the reconciliation of "all things, whether things on earth or things in heaven" (v. 20). Paul defines these "things" a few verses earlier as systems of power, "all things . . . whether thrones or powers or rulers or authorities," which he describes as "things in heaven and on earth, visible and invisible" (v. 16)—that is, the redemption of all "visible" systems of human rule "on earth," and of all "invisible" spiritual powers "in heaven."

These "principalities and powers" are part of the "dominion of darkness" (v. 14) from which humanity was redeemed, and which Paul tells

---

7. For a sociological study of this among conservative evangelicals, see Smith *American Evangelicalism*.

us will itself be redeemed. In this we see our understanding of salvation expanded beyond individual redemption, to the redemption of society and politics.[8]

Like us, the Powers were,

> **created good . . .** "in him all things were created: things in heaven and on earth, visible and invisible, whether thrones or powers or rulers or authorities; all things have been created through him and for him." (Col 1:16)

> **. . . are fallen . . .** "Our struggle is not against flesh and blood, but against the rulers, against the authorities, against the powers of this dark world and against the spiritual forces of evil in the heavenly realms." (Eph 6:12)

> **. . . and can be redeemed.** "For God was pleased to have all his fullness dwell in him, and through him to reconcile to himself all things, whether things on earth or things in heaven, by making peace through his blood, shed on the cross." (Col 1:19–20)[9]

In Jesus' teaching, Paul's concepts of "dominion of darkness" and the "kingdom of his Son" find a parallel in language of the "kingdom of God" in opposition to the "kingdom of Satan" or "the world" found in the Gospels. In his teaching of the way of the kingdom versus the way of the world, Jesus juxtaposes two diametrically opposed value systems. Especially in light of the violent reaction Jesus received from both religious and governmental authorities for these teachings, we can see that the kingdom of God confronts political, economic, social, institutional, and family structures. Walter Wink, who perhaps more than any other scholar of our time has plumbed the depths of New Testament teaching on systemic evil in his trilogy on the powers, writes,

> Not only did Jesus and his followers repudiate the autocratic values of power and wealth, but the institutions and systems that authorized and supported these values: the family, the law, the sacrificial system, the Temple, kosher food regulations, the distinction between clean and unclean, patriarchy, role expectations for women and children, the class system, the use of violence, racial

---

8. For an in-depth treatment of this, see Wink, *Engaging the Powers*. I cannot recommend this book highly enough. Wink's insights into the depths of human and demonic evil in the New Testament are unparalleled.

9. Wink, *Engaging the Powers*, 65–86.

and ethnic divisions, the distinction between insider and outsider—indeed, every conceivable prop of domination, division, and supremacy. The Gospel . . . is a context specific remedy for the evils of the Domination System.[10]

What Wink here calls the "Domination System" is the "way of the world" both in the times of kings and in our world today with its own share of war, terror, oppression, slavery, and sweatshops. This Domination System, run on oppression and violence, is far bigger than any CEO or Caesar. As Wink describes it, the system seems to take on a life of its own, corrupting, enslaving, and determining how we see ourselves, even determining *what* we can see, and what we can value.

As Wink demonstrates, the Domination System that enslaves us and crushes the human spirit is not some faceless impersonal monster. Rather the New Testament portrays it as something *we* are part of, something our sin creates, like an avalanche we set in motion. This tension between culpability and bondage found in scripture is often missed—conservatives emphasizing one side and liberals the other. Liberal Christians, for example, tend to underplay personal responsibility, blaming all evil on impersonal structures and systems. Conservatives, on the other hand, tend to ignore structural evil, believing that if individuals repent, the system will automatically change. But as we saw above, changed lives do not automatically change structural problems. Our societal, economic, and political structures need to be redeemed as well.

THE BIG PICTURE

A focus solely on individual redemption creates a kind of tunnel vision where we can only offer solutions that at best deal with the individual symptoms, rather than the larger disease which requires sociological, political, and economic change. Salvation entails our personal redemption, to be sure, but it entails much more. As Greg Boyd writes, "We simply cannot grasp the depth of the significance of the cross and resurrection so long as we restrict our perspective to what they accomplish for us."[11]

While penal substitution focuses almost exclusively on our individual salvation, Christus Victor understands our salvation within the larger

10. Ibid., 110.
11. Boyd, *God at War*, 251.

picture of a cosmic victory over evil. It is about our healing, and the healing of our world. This is tremendously significant because it means salvation is not simply a private religious affair, but entails putting all of life under Christ—our social, political, economic, national, and legal systems all need to reflect Christ's way. Christus Victor captures the full scope of the redemption of both us and our world, while penal substitution tends to limit salvation to privatized faith.

A second way that Christus Victor differs from penal substitution is its focus on Christ's triumph over the Domination System of abusive religious and political authority. Of all sins, the sin of abusive authority is particularly dangerous because it masquerades as righteousness, claiming to speak for God. History is crimson stained with examples of how abusive religious and political authority has been used to justify war, torture, and oppression—all in the name of God and justice. Exposing these false authorities is a central focus of how Christus Victor frames the work of Christ. In contrast, proponents of penal substitution seem to be completely unaware of this dynamic, seeing the law and authority as unquestioned standards that must be "satisfied," rather than brought under Christ. In its legal view, only individuals can transgress from the system, but the sins of systems—sins that have devastating effects on people's lives—are overlooked and even justified.

Because Christus Victor encompasses the full scope of salvation (entailing the redemption of fallen humanity and our fallen systems) it should not be reduced to one "motif" among many, but rather as the grand conceptual framework, the big picture of the full scope of God's salvation in Christ. Specifically, this narrative framework can be described as a *restorative model of salvation* (encompassing both our restoration and the restorations of our systems) *that exposes and overturns the fallen way of punitive justice.* The way of Christ overcomes the way of the law. Restoration triumphs over retribution. This is the central narrative of the New Testament. Both the positive focus on restoration, and negative focus on exposing and overturning the system of retribution are foundational here to a full understanding of the work of Christ.

7

INCARNATIONAL ATONEMENT

Vicarious Atonement as Participation in the Way of Christ

IN THIS CHAPTER WE will explore how the concept of Christ's death "for us" (an idea traditionally known as *vicarious* or *substitutionary* atonement) fits into the larger New Testament context of God's act of restorative justice in Christ. Substitutionary atonement is today usually associated with *penal* substitution. That is, it is assumed that the purpose of the substitution was punishment. However, this is not the only way to understand substitution. In fact, a careful reading of the works of the church fathers reveals that the early church did not understand substitution in terms of punishment, but rather in the context of Christus Victor's dual themes of healing and liberating humanity from sin and death. In other words, within a framework of restorative justice rather than retributive justice.[1]

For example, Athanasius writes, "The death of all was consummated in the Lord's body; yet, because the Word was in it, *death and corruption were in the same act utterly abolished.*"[2] Here we have substitutionary language, "the death of all was consummated in the Lord's body," understood in the context of Christus Victor, resulting in "death and corruption" being "utterly abolished." The death sentence is not fulfilled, it is erased. Atha-

---

1. For a detailed study of this, see my article "Substitutionary atonement and the Church Fathers."

2. Athanasius, *On the Incarnation*, 4. Emphasis added.

nasius writes that Christ "assumed a human body, in order that in it death might once for all be destroyed, and that men might be renewed according to the Image."[3] Note the dual themes of death's destruction and our renewal. Similarly, Gregory of Nazianzus writes, "For my sake he was called a curse, who destroyed my curse."[4] Again vicarious language (Christ cursed "for my sake") is coupled with a Christus Victor theme (the curse—that is, the sentence of the law—is "destroyed" not satisfied).

This language of death and curse being "abolished" and "destroyed," present in both Gregory and Athanasius, is quite significant. It begins with the assumption of validity of retributive justice: We are not only victims of Satan's bondage, we are also sinners and the just consequence of that is death. But in the Christ event (incarnation, crucifixion, resurrection) this way of retributive justice has been superseded, replaced and "destroyed" by the superior way of restorative justice. The law of sin and death is therefore overturned and abolished, replaced by the superior economy of grace, which works to set free and restore life.

Here the medical paradigm, prevalent among the church fathers, is helpful: Seen through the lens of the patristics' image of salvation as *healing*, we can think here of a doctor who, while recognizing that certain behaviors can lead to injury and sickness, nonetheless seeks to heal the patient. We have a grave wound, but Christ is a greater physician. As Augustine puts it, "Of my own so deadly wound I should despair, unless I could find so great a Physician!"[5] Punitive justice wounds, but restorative justice heals. The purpose of Christ's taking on human wretchedness, suffering, and sin, was for the sake of our healing and renewal.

This view of salvation as healing, sanctification, and re-creation is captured well by Gregory's well known formulation, "What is not assumed is not healed, but what is united to God is saved."[6] Christ's vicarious suffering is understood here in terms of God incarnationally entering into our human estate—embracing us even to the point of dying our death in order to overcome death and sin, and heal and renew us into God's image in Christ.

3. Athanasius, *On the Incarnation*, 13.

4. Gregory of Nazianzus, *Fourth Theological Oration*, Oration 30.

5. Augustine, *Exposition on the Psalms*, 51.6.

6. Gregory of Nazianzus, "To Cledonius Against Apollinaris" (Epistle 101.7). Quoted in Meyendorff, *Christ in Eastern Christian Thought*, 113. For the full text, see Hardy, *Christology of the Later Fathers*, 215–24.

This is an understanding of substitution which is largely unfamiliar to most Protestants, so it is important to see that the early church's understanding has a firm foundation in scripture. With this in mind, we turn to the following section to explore this concept in the letters of Paul.

INTERCHANGE IN CHRIST

It is important to note that theological terms such as *substitution, representational, vicarious,* and *satisfaction* never actually appear in the Bible. They are instead all attempts to describe what is meant by what the Bible does describe using little prepositions like *for, with,* and *in.* Paul says frequently that Christ died "*for us*" (Rom 5:8; Gal 3:13; Eph 5:2; 1 Thess 5:10). This clearly has the sense of benefaction done in solidarity and love. But does it carry the sense of Christ dying *instead of* us?

This interpretation is in fact ruled out because we are called to die "*with* Christ" (Rom 6:4–5; Gal 2:20; Col 2:12). Paul writes that because Christ "died for all, therefore *all died*" (2 Cor 5:14). This is not the idea of Christ dying instead of us, but rather of participation—Christ dies *and so do we.* Because of this, I prefer to use the term "vicarious suffering," which has come to imply that Christ died "for us," as opposed to "substitution," which in contrast is associated with penal substitution and thus taken to mean that Christ died "instead of us."[7]

Paul's full formula here is that we die with Christ in order to rise with Christ. Again, the model here is not substitution in the sense of a Christ dying *instead of* us, but rather of our *participation* in Christ,

> Or don't you know that all of us who were baptized into Christ Jesus were baptized into his death? . . . For if we have been united with him in a death like his, we will certainly also be united with him in a resurrection like his (Rom 6:3, 5).

---

7. This distinction reflects how these terms have come to be used by theologians. The etymological root meaning of these two terms is virtually synonymous. It is worth noting that many evangelical theologians, while using the term "substitution," do not intend it in a retributive sense, but rather in a vicarious sense (for us). A classic example of this is P.T. Forsyth (*The Work of Christ*). A more recent example is Colin Gunton (*The Actuality of Atonement*). N.T. Wright (somewhat confusingly) uses the term "penal substitution" while rejecting its Reformed understanding, apparently meaning vicarious suffering more generally (Wright, "The Cross and the Caricatures").

We read in 2 Timothy, "If we have died with him, we will also live with him" (2 Tim 2:11). The Greek here combines the prefex "with" (*syn*) with the verbs "to live" and "to die." If we *die-together* (*synapethanomen*) with Christ we will also *live-together* (*syzēsomen*) with him.[8] Here there is a sense of intimate union implied.

Perhaps the most powerful expression of this is Paul's statement that "God made him who had no sin to be sin for us, so that in him we might become the righteousness of God" (2 Cor 5:21). This is a passage that deserves to be looked at with great care: although Christ "has no sin" God made him "become sin." That is staggering: Paul does not say that Christ was made a "sinner" but that he was made to "be sin" itself. He did this *for us*, Paul writes, but to what end? Was it to satisfy the demands of retributive punishment, as penal substitution would assume? No, because, as Paul states, its purpose is so that "we might *become the righteousness of God.*" In other words, it is restorative not retributive. Christ was made *sin itself*, so we would be made *righteousness itself.*

How does this come about? Paul says here that we become the righteousness of God "in him" (2 Cor 5:21). This concept of our being "in Christ" is a phrase used frequently by Paul that speaks of our abiding in Christ, living *with him, in him, and through him* as new people. We are transformed into God's image (that is, into Christlikeness which is the image of God) through abiding fellowship, relational union, being *in* Christ. Spending time with Jesus in a loving and intimate personal relationship changes who we are.

There are two aspects of this that are important to note: First, the *means* by which we become righteous is through a living relationship with the indwelling Spirit of God. Second, the *goal* of this Spirit-led life is to reflect the image of Christ, to be Christ-like, to lead Jesus-shaped lives. Through a loving relationship with God, we are led by the Spirit into a life of Christ-like love. Both the *means* (a Spirit-led life) and the *goal* (Christlikeness) are crucial to understanding what Paul intends with his concept of being "in Christ." Put differently, his focus is clearly on cultivating a living personal relationship with God, but this not one that is myopically focused on our own personal salvation, but rather is focused on exhibiting Christlike love in all that we do, on becoming like Jesus.

8. See also Rom 6:6–8 where Paul speaks of us being "crucified-together" (synestaurōthē) with Christ and "living-together with/in him" (syzēsomen autō).

Morna Hooker has identified this process as "interchange in Christ."[9] It is succinctly stated in the classic formula of Irenaeus: *God became what we are, so we could become what he is* (i.e., Christ-like).[10] This "interchange" is rooted in the incarnation: God in Christ enters into our brokenness, stooping down to us in our need, as we participate through union with Christ ("with him" and "in him") we can share in God's incarnational death and resurrection.

Interchange is an idea that fit easily into the Hellenistic mindset of the early church fathers, but which has greatly troubled many modern Christians. Nineteenth-century church historian Adolf von Harnack disparagingly referred to the church fathers' presentation of this as a "physico-pharmacological" process, declaring it to be incomprehensible to the modern mind.[11] Others today similarly dismissively refer to it as a kind of "magic."

I'd like to suggest (much to Harnack's relief) that this idea in Paul is not nearly as esoteric as the patristic writers suggest, and in fact is quite down-to-earth and practical, having to do with our relationship with God. Paul picks up this theme in several of his letters (see Rom 8; 1 Cor 15; 2 Cor 1; 2 Cor 5; Eph 1). In particular, we can find a great deal of insight into this in Romans 8. There Paul compares our relationship with God to adoption, and argues that because we are "adopted sons" we are also "co-heirs with Christ" the Son, sharing in his inheritance of eternal life (Rom 8:15–17). Adoption here is both a legal term, having to do with rights (we are no longer "slaves," but are now "sons" who inherit), and at the same time a term of intimacy: Paul speaks here of how the indwelling Spirit testifies to our own spirits so that we know we are God's beloved children, and our hearts cry out "Abba, father!" (Rom 8:15).

That experience of the Spirit of God indwelling our hearts, Paul says, is the "firstfruits" of our participation in God's resurrection life. It is the "deposit, guaranteeing what is to come" (2 Cor 5:5). Just as the Spirit makes

---

9. Morna Hooker originally outlined the concept of "interchange" in *From Adam to Christ*, 13–72. It is also succinctly outlined in her *Paul: A Short Introduction*, 90–102. Hooker's term "interchange" is more specific than "vicarious" because it implies "with us" in addition to "for us."

10. "The Word of God, our Lord Jesus Christ, who did, through His transcendent love, become what we are, that He might bring us to be even what He is Himself" Irenaeus, *Against Heresies*, bk. 5, Preface.

11. von Harnack, *History of Dogma*, 238.

us alive now, even though we are still subject to sickness and death here, that same life-giving Spirit at work in us will also make us alive after death:

> You, however, are not in the realm of the flesh but are in the realm of the Spirit, if indeed *the Spirit of God lives in you* . . . But if *Christ is in you*, then even though your body is subject to death because of sin, *the Spirit gives life* because of righteousness. And if the Spirit of him who raised Jesus from the dead *is living in you*, he who raised Christ from the dead will also *give life* to your mortal bodies because of *his Spirit who lives in you*. (Rom 8:9–11)

We can see here that Paul describes our participation in Christ's resurrection power in very practical terms: we experience this through a vital and growing loving relationship with God active in our lives, which guarantees that this same Spirit dwelling in us will also give us eternal life.

Our experience of the reality of a loving relationship with God now—the experience of God's Spirit, active in us—constitutes the "firstfruits" pointing to the reality of an end to literal death, sickness, and suffering. This not only entails our individual redemption, Paul concludes, but the redemption of the whole creation (vv. 18–21). The "new birth" in us is the firstfruits of the new birth of all of creation. What we experience now in a loving personal relationship with Jesus Christ, leading us to walk in love, is the guarantee of what we do not experience yet—the end of suffering, sickness, injustice, and death. Therefore our participation in the death and resurrection of Christ—our dying with him so we can also live *with* and *in* him—is lived out within the very practical and tangible identity-forming experience of a personal relationship with God. Simply put, we give our lives to Jesus, and he lives in us. Because we belong to Jesus, what Jesus has is ours too. Participation is not "physico-pharmacological," it is *relational*.

8

THE SUFFERING SERVANT

Understanding Christ's Suffering in the Context of Injustice

IN THIS CHAPTER WE continue to explore the theme of Christ's vicarious suffering through a study of Isaiah's song of the Suffering Servant.

Judging by all the times the Servant Song is quoted or alluded to by the New Testament authors, it seems clear that it was pivotal in their understanding of Jesus' messianic work.[1] At the same time, it is widely agreed that the idea of a suffering messiah was utterly foreign to Judaism at the time.[2] This bears out in the reactions of the disciples themselves, who did not understand that the messiah "had to suffer," and even rebuked Jesus for suggesting it (Matt 16:13–23). The notion of a crucified messiah was therefore a "scandal," as Paul says (1 Cor 1:23). Seemingly aware of this shock, Isaiah opens the chapter with the words, "who can believe this?" (Isa 53:1, quoted in John 12:38).[3]

Our reading will look to Isaiah's tragic song of the Suffering Servant, with an eye towards retaining its scandal and shock. In this, it will differ

---

1. For a helpful overview see Stott, *Cross of Christ*, 145–46.

2. At the same time, the righteous suffering of the people was a common idea. The difference is that the messiah was conceived of as a military ruler who would free the people from suffering through war. See Wright, *Jesus and the Victory of God*, 579–84.

3. Author's translation. The NET notes here that, "The perfect has a hypothetical force in this rhetorical question. For another example, see Gen 21:7."

from how it is typically approached by critical biblical exegesis in two important ways.

First, we are not primarily interested in reading it in its original historical context (the typical focus of modern exegesis). Rather our goal is to discover what the New Testament authors saw when they read Isaiah 53 and applied it to the atonement, which they of course did in the context of Christ's death and resurrection. In particular, we are interested in seeing how the New Testament authors looked back to Isaiah 53 in order to understand Christ's suffering.

Secondly, we take a cue from Walter Brueggemann, who has suggested that Isaiah 53 in particular is best approached on its own terms, as dramatic poetry.[4] With that in mind, we will approach the text from a literary-rhetorical angle, paying attention to the force of its powerful imagery, immersing ourselves in its story and passion, and in so doing connect it to the passion of Christ.

THE SERVANT SONG AS TRAGEDY

In Isaiah's song we find the shocking model for *how* the Servant would bring about this liberating justice—again, not in the way of worldly revolutions through inflicting suffering on evildoers, but through taking the suffering of evildoers upon himself. The prelude to this begins with chapter 52 verses 13–15:

> See, my servant will act wisely;
> he will be raised and lifted up and highly exalted.
> Just as there were many who were appalled at him—
> his appearance was so disfigured beyond that of any human being
> and his form marred beyond human likeness (Isa 52:13–14).

Here Isaiah says: *Look at the Servant now, lifted up to the highest place of honor! But it wasn't always that way. At first everyone was appalled by him. He was beaten down so low we could hardly tell he was still human.*

> So will he sprinkle many nations,
> and kings will shut their mouths because of him.
> For what they were not told, they will see,
> and what they have not heard, they will understand (Isa 52:15).

4. Brueggemann, "Isaiah 40–66," 141.

But the powerful will clap their hands over their mouths and fall silent in shock: What was unheard of they will see. What they never imagined will be right there in front of them.

> Who has believed our message,
> and to whom has the arm of the Lord been revealed (53:1)?

Who can accept this way? Who would have ever thought that this is the form God's salvation would take? Who can comprehend it? Here Isaiah has set the stage for what is to come. He is preparing us for a shock. The way of God's saving power is not at all what we have expected. It is as if Isaiah says, "Forget what you think you know and listen to this . . ."

> He grew up before him like a tender shoot,
> and like a root out of dry ground.
> He had no beauty or majesty to attract us to him,
> nothing in his appearance that we should desire him (v. 2).

Insignificant, unnoticeable, a little weed in a dry field. The Servant didn't have the usual attributes that we think of as being pretty or impressive, and so we didn't notice the beauty there. *Like a wildflower in the forest, that we either walked past or trampled over. We didn't recognize that there was a treasure among us, and we treated it like trash.*

> He was despised and rejected by mankind,
> a man of suffering, and familiar with pain.
> Like one from whom people hide their faces
> he was despised, and we held him in low esteem (v. 3).

He suffers, but we do not see and do not care. He is the stranger in the night that we turn away. He is the least of these. "I was hungry and you gave me nothing, I was in need and you sent me away." Like Job's friends, we blamed him for his misfortune and "considered him stricken by God."

> Surely he took up our pain and bore our suffering,
> yet we considered him punished by God,
> stricken by him, and afflicted (v. 4).

We have here the image of one carrying the weight of the world on his shoulders, bearing in himself the suffering of a whole planet. A man broken . . . for us. *Truly, he carried our sorrows and mended our wounds. But we did not recognize this kindness. We didn't see it. He led the life of a servant, and because of that we thought he was nothing.*

> But he was pierced for our transgressions,
> he was crushed for our iniquities;
> the punishment that brought us peace was upon him,
> and by his wounds we are healed (v. 5).

Here we come to a point of realization: We thought it was the servant who was to blame, but now we see that it is because of us that he is suffering. He was pierced because of *our* sins. Notice the juxtaposition here to the previous verse, which speaks of infirmities and sorrow, and this verse, which speaks of transgression and iniquity. Together our full problem is described here as involving not only sin, but sickness and suffering as well. Notice too that the remedy here is restorative: by his wounds we are *healed*.

SEEING OURSELVES IN THE MOB

Many readers will be familiar with the interpretation that the penal substitution offers for this verse: The piercing and punishing of Christ is something that God ordered in order to be appeased. However, as we will see in the following verses, the suffering described here is *anything but just*. On the contrary, it is described as deeply tragic and unfair. The paradigm of legal appeasement simply does not fit with the tragic image of a miscarriage of justice that Isaiah is painting. I would like to suggest therefore that we think of this in a paradigm more fitting to the text—the context of self-sacrificing love. To illustrate this consider the following scenario:

A girl caught in an illicit affair is surrounded by an angry mob. Ugly faces spit self-righteous accusations and threats: "We don't want you in our town, whore!" The mood is violent and volatile. The crowd presses nearer. Someone shoves the girl and knocks her to the ground. Suddenly a man steps between her and the crowd and says, "If you want to hurt her, you'll have to go through me first." The man turns to her and says "Go now, run!" She begins to run, and as she looks around, she sees the man buried in a sea of fists and boots. He is motionless, but they go on hitting him. Later, when she goes to visit him in the hospital, the girl finds his once gentle face beaten beyond recognition.

Some of us may find ourselves reflected in that girl—kicked down by hatred and abuse, made to feel worthless; treated like garbage until we start to believe we really are. He suffered the punishment meant for us. He suffered standing up for the voiceless. Others may see themselves present in the self-righteous mob—in the middle of a ruthless and ugly crowd. Like Paul we were there seeing it all and approving (cf. Acts 8:1). He was pierced because of our hate. That hatred is what made him suffer. We can be separated from God and from Life either by hurtful things we do (like the mob) or by hurtful things done to us (like the girl).

Surely all our lives are a mixture of both. At times we are hurt, and at times we hurt others. We may find hatred overtaking us like the girl, or consuming us like the mob. In either case what is needed is for us to be liberated out of that world of hate. Salvation in this context is about being liberated out of the reign of hatred into God's Kingdom of compassion. What it is not about is placing God in the role of the mob demanding punishment.

It is not God who crushed the Servant, it was us—just as it was *for* us. Christ entered into our human condition, and bore the weight of both our hurtfulness and hurt. Christ died for sinners, but he also died for the poor, the least, the afflicted, and those who suffer injustice. He died for all who labor under the weight of sin, not in order to appease punishment, but in order to liberate us from the grip of violence, suffering, abuse, and injustice.

> We all, like sheep, have gone astray,
> each of us has turned to our own way;
> and the LORD has laid on him the iniquity of us all (v. 6).

Verses 5–6 above can also be translated from the Hebrew as "He was wounded *because of* our rebellious deeds, crushed *because of* our sins ... the LORD caused *the sin of us all to attack him*" (NET). Similarly the Greek in the LXX can be similarly read "he was wounded *because of* our acts of lawlessness and has been weakened *because of* our sins . . . the Lord *gave him over to our sins*" (NETS). If these recent scholarly translations are correct, it would mean that it is our sin which "punishes" the servant. This coincides with the Gospel writers' presentation of the crucifixion of Jesus where it is the people, acting unjustly in the name of religious and civil power, who unjustly punished Jesus. In other words, the Servant did not suffer because God demanded a punishment, but because hatred did. God was given over to all the hatred and wrath of the world, and the stress Isaiah puts on this is that it was *our* hatred and wrath.

UNMASKING RELIGIOUS VIOLENCE

Unmasking religiously justified violence is a major theme of Girardian atonement theories, and this is clearly a key focus in Isaiah 53. God shows solidarity with all victims in identifying with the Servant. At the same time, it is critical to notice that the "we" of Isaiah 53 is directed to the *victimizers*, who are confronted with their sin. In other words, this is not only good news for the oppressed, it is good news for sinners. The ones who are "healed" in Isaiah's narrative are the ones who have hurt. That healing involves our repentance, away from the way of retribution, and towards the Servant's way of enemy love.

In this, we move beyond typical Girardian theory, which tends to focus solely on the unmasking of sanctified violence, and towards healing and redeeming sinners—sinners hiding under a mantle of self-righteousness. It exposes our hate masquerading as piety, and shows a way to be righteous based on radical mercy. God, in identifying with the Servant, rejects the way of retribution—the way of the mob—and instead endorses the way of the Servant. The Servant's story is therefore an indictment against the injustice of retribution.

> He was oppressed and afflicted, yet he did not open his mouth;
> he was led like a lamb to the slaughter,
> and as a sheep before her shearers is silent, so he did not open his mouth.
> By oppression and judgment he was taken away (vv. 7–8a).

By oppression and judgment he was taken away. The NRSV renders this, "By a perversion of justice he was taken away." We get the sense here that we are witnesses to something tragic, something terribly unfair, and indeed we should. This was not about the fulfillment of the righteous requirement of the Law, but as the text says, it is about a "perversion of justice." It was oppression and judgment crushing love. As with the man in the story above who suffered the wrath of that angry mob, the context of Isaiah 53 makes it quite clear that the punishment—the painful consequence that the Servant endures—is undeserved and unjust. It is a miscarriage of justice, not its fulfillment. Again, this mirrors what we find in the Gospels, where the death of Jesus is likewise portrayed as a miscarriage of justice.

There is a tendency in our effort to understand the cross to take the isolated formulations in Isaiah 53 and plug them into a sort of equation for the mechanics of the atonement. In doing this we can easily end up with a formula of the Servant being legally punished in the place of sinners to satisfy the demands of punitive justice. But in removing these sayings from their original context, and inserting them into a rational formula, we do violence to Isaiah's intent. If we want to understand what Isaiah is saying, then we need to read it within the narrative framework that the story provides. What we see in the Servant Song is not the picture of the fulfillment of justice but rather the unmasking of a grave injustice.

> Yet who of his generation protested?
> For he was cut off from the land of the living;
> for the transgression of my people he was punished (v. 8).

Notice that we find here clear punitive elements as the means of our atonement—his *punishment* brought us peace, by his *stripes* we are healed—but all in the context of unjust suffering. It is a picture of *unjust* penal substitution. Recognizing this tension is critical: God brings about justice by submitting to profound injustice. The victory is won by Jesus *losing* his life. God triumphs over our evil by entering into our failure, shame, and affliction. Because of this, the very cycle of violence and dominance is overturned. It is a triumph over triumphalism, the conquest of conquest.

> He was assigned a grave with the wicked, and with the rich in his death,
> though he had done no violence, nor was any deceit in his mouth (v. 9).

Jesus was stripped naked as a common criminal and "numbered among the transgressors," even though "he had done no violence, nor was any deceit in his mouth." Because of this, the injustice of the mob was exposed. Rome crucified Christ as a common criminal to show that no one can oppose the System. But as Love hung on that cross, the authorities were exposed, unmasked in their hatred. Paul tells us that Christ "made a public spectacle" of the powers and authorities on the cross (Col 2:15). The mob had their own sin laid in front of them like the lamb on the altar.

In a sense all of Isaiah 53 can be seen as a lament, as a tragedy, similar to the prophetic Psalms of David that point to Christ, "My God, my God, why have you forsaken me? . . . I am poured out like water, and all my bones are out of joint. My heart has turned to wax; it has melted within me" (Ps 22:1, 14). But unlike many Psalms, this is more than a lament for an individual. It is a lament with the specific purpose of appealing to the conscience of its audience. Throughout the chapter, Isaiah returns to the theme of realization that while we considered the Servant stricken by God, it was *our* sickness, *our* sorrow, and *our* sin on his back. The point of view through which this tragic drama is viewed is through the eyes of the mob, realizing that what we have done is horribly wrong. We thought he must have been guilty, Isaiah says, but in fact it was we who are guilty, we who are afflicted.

Through a confrontation with the accursedness of the Servant, Isaiah confronts us with our own accursedness. The song of the Suffering Servant is thus a call to repentance, but what is vital to notice is what precisely we are being called repent *of: We are called to repent of religiously justified hatred and violence*. It is an indictment of our own religious judgmentalism and hatred. Like the message of Jesus in the Gospels, which calls us to turn away from the way of judgment and to embrace instead the way of radical mercy, Isaiah calls us to embrace the way of the Servant. We are confronted with our ugliness and hatefulness, and at the same time we see that God incarnate, rather than coming in wrath, is bearing that hurt *for us*. The mask of our self-righteousness is pulled away; the sin of the entire system of retributive justice is exposed; and simultaneously we see that the Servant has endured our injustice in order to heal us. It is a message intended to bring us to our knees, and the very system of retribution along with it.

THE INJUSTICE OF SUBSTITUTION

Isaiah stresses over and over again how shocking and unfair the plight of the Servant is, how hard it is to comprehend. We are confronted with the horror of unjust suffering, and like the disciples, the appropriate and normal response is to flee. But despite that shock, despite the seeming injustice, God has a plan in this darkness. God will use this evil and turn it to good. God will take the injustice of a Roman cross and use it to bring about our justification.

Yet it was the LORD's will to crush him and cause him to suffer,
and though the LORD makes his life an offering for sin,
he will see his offspring and prolong his days,
and the will of the LORD will prosper in his hand (v. 10).

Martin Luther, commenting on Isaiah 53, remarks how utterly foreign such an idea is to any conceivable legal perspective: "Natural reason, divine as well, argues that everybody must bear their own sin. Yet he is struck down contrary to all law and custom."[5] So how then are we to process the scandal of the cross? Luther continues, "Therefore the prophet leads us so earnestly beyond all righteousness and our rational capacity and confronts us with the sufferings of Christ . . . This is the preaching of the whole Gospel, to show us that Christ suffered for our sake contrary to law, right, and custom"[6] Christ suffered for our sake *contrary to law, right, and custom.*

This brings out an element of penal substitution that is not often acknowledged: Even within its own rational judicial framework it is simply not just to punish the innocent for the sake of the guilty. There is simply no government or legal system in the world that would claim this. Regardless of whether the purpose of punishment is thought to be for reform, protection, or even vengeance—no legal system operates by taking the life of an innocent person in the place of a guilty one. The only possible way to miss this rather glaring point is to think in the most detached mathematical terms possible, where a life is abstractly given a certain value or "merit" and the exchange of a more valuable life "balances the books." This so-called "reason" is blinded to the obvious fact that this would be extremely unjust according to the standards of any criminal justice system.

Proponents of penal substitution have attempted to surmount this by saying that God does not punish an innocent third party, but bears the punishment himself. It is true enough that God was in Christ on the cross, but this does not change the fact that it is not a fulfillment of justice to punish the innocent, even if it is voluntary. God bearing the weight of our sin is not just or reasonable, it is scandalous, unmerited grace. There is no economy of justice where this would be considered a reasonable exchange. Thus as Luther says, to understand what Isaiah is saying, we need to go beyond any sort of reasonable and rational understandings of legal exchange. Grace bursts all categories of reasonableness or requirement.

5. *Luther's Works*, Vol. 17, 221, commentary on Isaiah 53.
6. Ibid., 222.

Now while in a legal context it is simply unheard of for the innocent to be punished in the place of the guilty, in a relational context it is often the case that the innocent bear the weight of the sins of the guilty out of love. Take for example a family where the mother is addicted to prescription medication: The family may suffer the consequences of her addiction far more profoundly than she does, precisely because they are good. Their goodness means they see and suffer the brokenness in her life much more than she does in her dulled state of denial. They suffer willingly because they have bound themselves to her in love. Likewise, Jesus—in identifying himself with sinful humanity—suffers under that weight, the innocent bearing the weight of the sins of the guilty. That which in a legal paradigm is a travesty of justice becomes in a relational paradigm a picture of the suffering love of solidarity and compassion. As the family bears the sin of that mother in her afflictions, they are afflicted. In the same way Christ bears our sin in love.

Isaiah paints this story for us from the perspective of the mob, and the result is that in the Servant unjustly bearing suffering, our injustice is exposed in the same way the civil rights protesters exposed the injustice of racial hatred. Martin Luther King describes how the bearing of unjust suffering acts not only to expose the injustice of the system, but to convert those behind it as well:

> Send your hooded perpetrators of violence into our community at the midnight hour and beat us and leave us half dead, and we shall still love you. But be ye assured that we will wear you down by our capacity to suffer . . . We shall so appeal to your heart and conscience that we shall win you in the process and our victory will be a double victory.[7]

If a nonviolent civil rights protestor is beaten by the police, this acts to unmask the injustice of the system. We would not, however, say that the police officer is right in striking them, as if they were fulfilling some necessary function. It is not the evil act of abusive authority which is redemptive, it is the response of the protestor who does not retaliate, who breaks the cycle of violence. The Servant is the one whose act redeems by unmasking our sin masquerading as religiously justified violence.

What Isaiah 53 shows is the power of love of enemies in action. When Isaiah writes "yet it was the Lord's will" for the Servant to suffer, this must be understood in the same way that the Gospels also frame the death of

7. King, *King Came Preaching*, 178.

Christ as being unjust, and yet the will of both the Son and the Father. Not because God demands retribution and thus becomes a member of the mob, but because God is the Servant and uses our evil in order to overcome evil with good.

THE LYNCHPIN OF THE ATONEMENT

From our study of Isaiah 53 thus far we can see that vicarious suffering can indeed be seen as the central mechanism, the lynchpin, of the atonement. However, what we especially see in Isaiah's tragic song is that this incarnational *participation* does not operate on the principle of retributive justice, but rather is based on the principle of restorative justice and enemy love. That is, the purpose of the Servant's vicarious suffering is to *heal* us (restorative justice), and this is done in the context of loving us despite our sin and injustice in falsely condemning and crushing the Servant (enemy love). As a result, the suffering of the Servant not only acts to reveal our sin of religious violence, but also acts to unmask the very system of retributive justice itself.

This constitutes a judgment of both our religious violence and the system of violence that calls itself justice, rather than the satisfaction of that system. It is an indictment of punishment that seeks to *heal* through bearing unjust suffering vicariously: "By his stripes we are *healed*." This is vicarious atonement understood within the context of restorative justice. This indictment of the very system of retributive justice becomes especially clear in the light of the resurrection, which acts to undo the death sentence of the crucifixion. Just as the resurrection follows Christ's death, Isaiah's poem also ends with the raising of the Servant:

> After he has suffered, he will see the light of life and be satisfied;
> by his knowledge my righteous servant will justify many,
> and he will bear their iniquities (v. 11).

Here we are taken out of the realm of the sacrificial ritual because the sacrifices acted to restore a person into the law, but resurrection acts to undo the verdict of the Servant's executioners. As a result, the very system of justice that accused him is called into question: "By a perversion of justice he was taken away" (Isa 53:8, NRSV). For this reason, when the death of Christ is spoken of as a "sacrifice" we must understand this in the context in which it is framed by both the Gospels and Isaiah 53—in the context of unjust suffering acting to unmask and redeem the sins of violence and condemnation masquerading as justice.

GOD IS THE SUFFERING SERVANT

In the Suffering Servant, we have a picture of God identifying with the victim, the condemned, the accursed. With that context in mind let's take another look at this classic text from Isaiah 53:

> Surely he took up our pain and bore our suffering, yet we considered him punished by God, stricken by him, and afflicted. But he was pierced for our transgressions, he was crushed for our iniquities; the punishment that brought us peace was on him, and by his wounds we are healed. (Isa 53:4–5)

This verse is commonly used as a proof-text for penal substitution, but notice first of all that Isaiah speaks of the Servant not only bearing our sin, but also bearing our *sickness*. In fact, the Gospel of Matthew directly connects this verse with the healing ministry of Jesus "He took up our infirmities and bore our diseases" (Matt 8:17). The second Hebrew word here, translated in the NIV as "suffering," carries the sense of mental anguish and grief, "Surely he hath borne our griefs, and carried our sorrows" (KJV). What we have here, in the rich and nuanced language of Isaiah, is a complex picture—not only of Christ bearing the weight of our sin—but also bearing the weight of our hopelessness, woundedness, and grief.

This gets at the deeper conception of sin we explored in chapter 3, which goes beyond simply understanding our brokenness in terms of legal transgression and towards an understanding of how we can also be cut off and alienated through suffering, tragedy, and pain. Jesus died in order to break past everything that can separate us from God and life—whether that is guilt, tragedy, sorrow, self-hatred, illness, disability, doubt, oppression, or abuse.

Christ took up our iniquities, yes. But he also bore our sorrow and infirmities. Jesus bore the pain of every victim of rape, torture, and abuse. He was crushed for all those who have been crushed by disappointment or grief. He was broken for every broken heart, and is there in the darkness with everyone whose hope is lost. Christ bore on the cross all of our failure, pain, guilt, helplessness, sickness, and despair. Christ bore the just consequences of sin—and the unjust consequences of sin as well. On the cross God took on the full effect of sin and evil in the world, so that nothing would separate us from God's love. Christ enters into our doubt, abandonment, pain, lostness, and grief so that with, in, and through Christ we can rise to new life in the middle of a dark world.

GOD'S WAY OF SUFFERING-LOVE

Isaiah's song, which began in failure and disdain, now ends in triumph as the way of the Servant is vindicated.

> Therefore I will give him a portion among the great,
> and he will divide the spoils with the strong,
> because he poured out his life unto death,
> and was numbered with the transgressors.
> For he bore the sin of many,
> and made intercession for the transgressors. (v. 12)

One could initially get the impression here that the point of suffering is simply to endure so we can receive a reward later—as if it were an extreme form of "work hard so you can get to the top." I would like to propose, however, that there is something deeper going on: *The act of other-directed love expressed in humility and dying to self is what leads to glorification.* We can see this illustrated by comparing the transformation we see in the Suffering Servant to a parallel account in the Christ hymn in Paul's letter to the Philippians. As with Isaiah's song, Paul's hymn begins in lowliness,

> Christ Jesus: Who, being in very nature God . . . *made himself nothing, by taking the very nature of a servant*, being made in human likeness. And being found in appearance as a man, *he humbled himself and became obedient to death—even death on a cross!* (Phil 2:5–8)

Jesus, whom the creeds proclaim as "very God of very God," humbled himself, came and served, associating with the lowliest and the unclean, washing the feet of his disciples, and then endured a profoundly humiliating, shameful death: stripped naked, he became accursed in our place—for love, for us.

The root Greek word that Paul uses here which is translated as "made himself nothing" in the NIV or in the RSV as "emptied himself" is the verb *kenoō*, from which we derive our English word "kenosis" (Greek: *kenōsis*). In the past theologians have used this verse to contemplate the mechanics of how exactly the Divine would take the form of a fallible man. God "emp-ties himself" in order to be poured into a human vessel. In so doing, how-ever, past theologians missed the central message of this hymn, which is about God's way—the poured out life, the way of Kenosis.[8]

Paul's main point in the context of this passage in Philippians is to encourage the believers to be imitators of Christ's humility, to take on the same servant life that Jesus did. Paul describes a few verses later this pattern of servanthood in his own life, "Even if I am being poured out like a drink offering on the sacrifice and service coming from your faith, I am glad and rejoice with all of you" (Phil 2:17). Paul's language of being "poured out" as he follows in the footsteps of Jesus echoes the language of Isaiah "because he poured out his life unto death" (53:12). Paul goes on to explain how he has given up privilege and rank in order to take on Christ's way of kenosis.

> If someone else thinks they have reasons to put confidence in the flesh, I have more: circumcised on the eighth day, of the people of Israel, of the tribe of Benjamin, a Hebrew of Hebrews; in regard to the law, a Pharisee; as for zeal, persecuting the church; as for righteousness based on the law, faultless.
> But whatever were gains to me I now consider loss for the sake of Christ. What is more, I consider everything a loss because of the surpassing worth of knowing Christ Jesus my Lord, for whose sake I have lost all things. I consider them garbage, that I may gain Christ. (Phil 3:4–8)

Here Paul is juxtaposing the way of the law and status with the way of the cross and kenosis. Two verses later we see a statement that is critical in understanding Paul's view of the cross:

> I want to know Christ—yes, to know the power of his resurrec-tion and participation in his sufferings, becoming like him in his death, and so, somehow, attaining to the resurrection from the dead. (Phil 3:10)

The fellowship of sharing in his sufferings. The pattern of *kenosis* we see emerging here—both in Paul's description of Christ, and in Paul's own imitation—is that of *status-humiliation-exaltation*.[9] Like Christ, Paul aban-

8. For a detailed study of the way of kenosis in the Philippian hymn and its meaning, both in terms of the way of Jesus and our way see Gorman, *Cruciformity*, 75–94, and *Inhabiting the Cruciform God*, 9–39.

9. Gorman identifies a similar pattern of *status—renunciation, abasement—resurrec-tion/exultation* (*Cruciformity*, 88–91).

dons his religious *status* and takes up *humiliation* in the hopes of being *raised* with Christ. The way of loving our enemies, dying to self, the way of the cross, transforms both our own lives and those around us and breaks the destructive cycle of sin and hostility. It is the way of kenosis itself that brings about the transformation. The Servant is exalted, we are told, *"because* he poured out his life unto death"* (Isa 53:12).

It is the poured-out way that leads to exaltation. Through the way of the cross, what was broken is made glorious. The pattern of *status-humiliation-exaltation* does not mean that one leaves their status, is humiliated, and as a reward is exalted, but that *the way of humility* itself is the exalted way that leads to glory. Jesus was not formerly a servant, and now a Lord. He is the Servant Lord. He is Lord *because* of his servanthood. "Anyone who wants to be first must be the very last, and the servant of all" (Mark 9:35). Commenting on Philippians 2:5–11, Morna Hooker writes,

> Christ did not cease to be "in the form of God" when he took the form of a slave. On the contrary, it is *in his self-emptying and humiliation that he reveals what God is like*, and it is through his taking the form of a slave that we see "the form of God."[10]

Because the New Testament understands the suffering servant as a picture of Christ, it is fundamentally *a picture of the nature and way of God*, revealed in the incarnation. God is the suffering servant and the way of kenosis is God's way. In showing love for us by dying for us while we were enemies, God breaks the enmity in us through the way of grace and kenosis—with unmerited kindness, returning love for our hate.

THE IMITATION OF CHRIST

In this and the previous chapter we have explored the concept of vicarious suffering understood in the context of restorative justice. This has taken shape through two major motifs: Isaiah's picture of the suffering servant, and Paul's concept of interchange. Put differently, the interpretation of Isaiah 53 offered here is essentially a Girardian one, the focus being on unmasking religious violence on a structural and systemic level. Interchange, on the other hand, is focused on inner moral transformation through relational union.

---

10. Hooker, *The Letter to the Philippians*, 508. Emphasis in original.

Both of these together—the personal and the social—are important for grasping the full picture of the role Christ's vicarious suffering has in our salvation. Interchange means we die with Christ (that is, we take on the way of suffering-love modeled by Christ) in order to rise with him, and takes place through participation—a living relationship with God transforming us into Christ-likeness. Likewise, the Servant models for us God's way of self-sacrificing enemy love that exposes and overcomes our injustice, and unmasks the way of retribution. In this, God in Christ models for us a new way that we are to follow, the way of the Servant.

Our following in this way however brings up a potential problem: How are we to distinguish between healthy and unhealthy forms of self-sacrificing love? When is it wrong, or even abusive, to endure suffering in love? As Walter Wink writes, "Nothing is deadlier to the spirit of Jesus' teaching on nonviolence than regarding it legalistically."[11] Our dying "with Christ," should not be understood as self-abnegation. Recall that the pattern of the Philippian Christ-hymn is status-humiliation-exaltation. One can only sacrifice what they have. One must possess power and status in order to relinquish it in love for the sake of the weak and needy. A person however who has not developed a healthy sense of self cannot be asked to give what they do not possess. *Self-sacrificing love must come from a position of strength.*

Secondly, the concept of self-sacrificing love needs to be understood within a relational context. In other words, the point is not to deny the self, so much as it is to move beyond self-focus towards a relational focus. Our identity is not autonomous, but relational. Developing into a social being begins with a healthy self-love formed in relationship, and in its mature form develops into expressions of self-sacrificing love, such as the love a parent gives a young child (as any exhausted parent of a newborn can tell you, parental love is sacrificial). At the same time it is crucial to remember that we are also part of the "we," and therefore need to exercise self-care in this as well (a truth we parents can often forget). Again, out of a basis of strength and maturity this "we-orientation" may thus entail making sacrifices in caring for others who are weaker.

Finally, self-sacrificing love does not seek suffering, rather it works to end it. Recall that the picture of the suffering servant is one of *exposing and unmasking* injustice, not of condoning or accepting it. Suffering is not

---

11. Wink, *Engaging the Powers*, 189.

good, love is. Love entails suffering because love entails making oneself vulnerable to the needs and hurts of others.

Our model for this servant life is God. God is the Servant. God is the one who comes to us in our need, in the middle of our grief. God is the one who enters into the place where the world is hurting and through taking on suffering, overcomes it; and God is the one who calls us to follow in the way of servant-love.

9

THE THEOLOGY OF THE CROSS

God's Saving Act in the Midst of Human Injustice

LET'S TAKE A MOMENT to take stock, and look at where we have come so far: Throughout this book I have argued for an understanding of the atonement based on restorative justice rather than retributive justice. This understanding combines Christus Victor and vicarious suffering together within that model of restorative justice and nonviolence.

The atonement is not simply about reconciliation, but about *regeneration*. This new birth is not a one-time event, but is the beginning of a formative relationship with the indwelling Spirit of Christ whose love transforms us into Christ-likeness. Being "saved" entails knowing Jesus relationally, and thus becoming like Jesus. Again, this is not simply about imitation of a standard or way, it is a matter of relational formation through the indwelling Spirit. Ethics is inseparably tied together here with soteriology. That is, it is through a loving and active relationship with the Spirit of Christ that we are formed into Christ-likeness.

The focus here has been on how salvation works in our lives: it is restorative, and works through a life-changing relationship with God. What we have not yet addressed is how this connects to the cross. Why did Jesus die? How does this heal us? These questions will be the focus of this chapter.

THE SCANDAL OF THE CROSS

Looking at the passion of Christ means facing the actual death of Jesus. We should be wary of any theory of the cross that removes this passion and shock, making it either "self-evident" (like a rational legal theory can), or "romanticizing" the crucifixion into palatable and noble metaphors (as both the Christus Victor and moral influence theory can). Any metaphors and meaning we might see in the cross are not abstract images. They refer to the very real death of Jesus—to Christ's shameful execution on a Roman cross. That is a reality that, if we take it seriously, should disturb us. As Jürgen Moltmann writes, "Christians who do not have the feeling that they must flee the crucified Christ have probably not yet understood him in a sufficiently radical way."[1]

In our world where there is no public crucifixion, and instead a cross is a smooth, clean symbol hanging on a wall or worn as a necklace, it is easy to forget how horrific the actual cross must have been. Historian Martin Hengel describes Roman crucifixion as "a form of execution which manifests the demonic character of human cruelty and bestiality."[2] It was, Hengel says, a cruel, barbaric, and shameful form of execution too crass for Romans to speak of, and considered an abomination by Jews. This was

1. Moltmann, *The Crucified God*, 38.
2. Hengel, *Crucifixion in the Ancient World*, 87.

the historical context of the "scandal" of the cross that Paul speaks of. This is what he means when he speaks of the cross being "a stumbling block to Jews, and foolishness to Gentiles" (1 Cor 1:23). Their objection was based on knowing full well exactly what a Roman cross meant. To truly understand the cross, we need to view it within its historical reality, which at first sight appears to be its foolishness, folly, and failure.

As Hengel explains, the cross was a form of execution in Rome primarily for rebels and slaves in order to shame and intimidate the lower classes and secure the authority of the Roman state. Within the Jewish context of the writers of the New Testament, Rome represented pagan oppression, not justice. Crucifixion, as practiced by Rome, was by no means a picture of the "fulfillment of justice" in the minds of the Jewish people, nor was it a symbol of "victory" for that matter. The cross was a symbol of shame and failure and accursedness—a terrible sign of defeat, not of victory. If we want to understand the reality of the cross, that is where we need to begin.

The New Testament presents the crucifixion as an act of human injustice. Jesus cries out from the cross, "Father, forgive them, for they do not know what they are doing" (Luke 23:34). Paul states that "None of the rulers of this age understood it, for if they had, they would not have crucified the Lord of glory" (1 Cor 2:8). The death of Christ was an act of human injustice, which Peter says was done "in ignorance" by "wicked men" (Acts 3:17 and 2:23). God's response, Peter says, was not to declare that justice had been satisfied, but to overturn that unjust verdict by raising Christ from the dead. Peter declares, "You killed the author of life, but God raised him from the dead" (Acts 3:15). That is, the death of Jesus was not God's act, it was an act of human injustice. Human hatred, sin, condemnation, and injustice killed Jesus.

Jesus did not want to die. He prayed through tears in the garden that the cup would be taken from him. In the same way, it did not please God the Father to watch his beloved Son die. As any father would, he died too that day. As Moltmann puts it, God the Father died to his fatherhood when he lost his only Son.[3] Yet at the same time Scripture says that the cross was the will of God the Father, "not my will, but yours be done" (Luke 22:42), as well as the will of the Son—"no one takes my life from me but I lay it down" (John 10:18). How are we to understand this apparent contradiction?

Speaking on the day of Pentecost, Peter proclaims, "This man was handed over to you by God's deliberate plan and foreknowledge; and you,

---

3. Moltmann, *Crucified God*, 243.

with the help of wicked men, put him to death by nailing him to the cross. But God raised him from the dead" (Acts 2:23–24). Note that we have Peter's same formula as above: human injustice overturned by God's vindication, but here it is all framed as part of God's ultimate plan. What happened to Jesus was horribly unjust, and yet it was how God brought about justice. It was wrong, but God entered into that wrongness and turned it around to make things right.

This is the great reversal of the cross. God enters into our darkness and makes justice come about despite injustice. God chose to make something good out of something bad. This does not mean that God condones evil and pain, but that God *overcomes* evil with good. It means that God can enter into all of our ugliness, evil, and hurt, and turn it around.

God did not demand the death of Jesus. In the Gospel narratives it was the people who cried out, *crucify, crucify!* It was human injustice and sin that demanded Christ's death. What God "demands" from all of us is love. Jesus chose to love, regardless of the cost, and that way of radical love in the midst of human sin inevitably led to him being unjustly condemned and killed by sinful humanity. As Daniel Migliore writes,

> It was divine "necessity"—the necessity of God's gracious and non-coercive love—that the love of God be fully expressed in all its vulnerability in Jesus Christ. It was human "necessity"—the necessity of the world order of our own making—that this one who mediated God's forgiveness and inaugurated the reign of God characterized by justice, freedom, and peace should become the victim of our violence because he threatened the whole world of violence that we inhabit and will to maintain.[4]

THE TWO ACTS OF GOD

The Roman cross was an act of human evil, injustice, and brutality. In contrast, the acts of God were the *incarnation* and the *resurrection*. The incarnation is God's shocking "Yes!" to fallen humanity. The resurrection is God's defiant "No!" to sin and death, both in term of the hurt done to us and the hurt we do.

In the incarnation God in Christ entered into our wretched, broken, sinful estate, into the depth of our sickness. Because God would not leave

---

4. Migliore, *Faith Seeking Understanding*, 189.

us alone in our darkness, because he would not forsake us in our sin, in Christ God entered into our "body of death," into a world filled with abuse, oppression, and injustice. In placing himself in solidarity with the poor and the least, Jesus made himself vulnerable to that same abuse and injustice. God's act in Christ was to enter into our lostness, uniting himself with the oppressed, the forsaken, and the forgotten, making himself vulnerable through love to the same forces of hatred, oppression, and violence that crush the least.

What God embraces in the incarnation is not death or suffering, rather God embraces us in our oppression, suffering, and brokenness. God's full embrace of humanity in the incarnation led God in Christ to the cross.

From this we can see why God chose the cross (the *motivation*): He chose to be faithful to love, regardless of the cost. We also know why Jesus died (the *cause*): Because *our* sin, hate, and disease killed him. Yet from these explanations alone we are still left with the question of *efficacy*: How does Christ dying in the name of love result in our sanctification and healing? How is it any different from the noble death of any other human dying for their beliefs and for the sake of others? When another person dies to protect others, or loses their life in the name of freedom, this may move and inspire us deeply, but as good and noble as this may be, it does not mean we would see their death as bringing about salvation of humanity. So what is different about Christ's death?

The answer is found in the two acts of God: the incarnation and resurrection. First, his death is different from all others because he alone rose from the dead, conquering death itself. Second, his life is different from all others because he alone was God incarnate, standing in the place of humanity.

The incarnation and resurrection are inseparably tied together here: If one person overcame death, this would benefit them alone. We would still need to face death on our own. However, because Christ took on our humanity in the incarnation, we can participate in his death, and likewise in his overcoming of death in the resurrection. It is *through* Christ taking on our humanity in the incarnation that we can participate in the saving power of the resurrection.

God through the incarnation fully embraces us in our brokenness and darkness, even to the point of suffering an unjust death on a cross. Rising from the dead, God makes a new way for us to participate in God's life in a loving personal relationship that changes us into Christ's image. The reality of that transformative relationship—of the Spirit active and alive in us—is the guarantee that we will also inherit eternal life, overcoming literal sickness and death (2 Cor 5:5).

The resurrection of Jesus thus acts like a window opened up in heaven letting God's reality burst into our gray world—like an anchor for our soul, holding us to Love, connecting our hearts with God's heart (cf. Heb 6:19). God's love is stronger than our evil, and the evil in our world. One day the whole world will be redeemed from evil and injustice. We are the first fruits of that total redemption, Christ living in our hearts as a proof of that promise. That foretaste should make us hungry for more, hungry to see not only others transformed by the love of God, but also to see our world and its structures and systems transformed by grace. We long for the resurrection of all things, the transformation of our lives and of society into God's reign of compassion. We long for an end to suffering and death. But we do this knowing the outcome is clear: Satan has been dealt the death blow through the cross and resurrection. Love is stronger than death.

The two acts of God were the incarnation and the resurrection. The incarnation entails Christ's death, but death is not the focus—solidarity with us in our sin and suffering is the focus. God's first act of embrace leading to the crucifixion meets God's second act in the resurrection where the unjust verdict of the cross is overturned, and death itself is overcome, making the way for us to enter into new life in Christ. Hebrews says that Jesus "endured the cross, scorning its shame" because of the "joy set before him" (Heb 12:2). That joy was the salvation which was won as he rose with the keys to death and hell. Death does not save; rather, Christ's *vicariously overcoming* our death in the resurrection does.

Note here how different all this is from penal substitution where the resurrection plays virtually no role. In fact, one might conclude that the resurrection undoes the entire punitive verdict that was supposed to appease God's wrath by punishing Jesus. Indeed this is *precisely* what the resurrection does—it undoes the judgment of death. Because the pivotal point of salvation is the resurrection, the purpose of the atonement is about overcoming and ending suffering through the resurrection. Death and suffering are conquered, not satisfied.

THE THEOLOGY OF THE CROSS

With this background in mind, it is not hard to understand why there is a tendency among today's proponents of Christus Victor to focus only on the resurrection, and leave out the cross. If indeed the cross itself was an act of human injustice, and the saving act of God is found in overcoming death in the resurrection, shouldn't we place our focus there?

Here we need to listen to the caution of Martin Luther, who was himself one of the most powerful advocates of Christus Victor. Nevertheless, Luther insists in bold letters, *CRUX sola est nostra theologia,* "the CROSS alone is our theology!"[5] Paul likewise tells the church in Corinth, "I resolved to know nothing while I was with you except Jesus Christ and him crucified" (1 Cor 2:2). Why is it so critical to Luther and Paul that we focus on the *"cross alone"*? Surely this does not mean that we must understand everything in the context of injustice. So what does it mean for Luther and Paul to view everything from the foot of the cross?

The cross is understood here as central *precisely* because it is paradoxical. The cross is the last place you would expect to find anything good. It represents injustice, pain, and death. Yet it is the shame, horror, and godlessness of the cross that leads to the resurrection. The way to life is through the cross, through death, damnation, and godforsakenness. As Jürgen Moltmann writes so poignantly, "God is not greater than he is in this humiliation. God is not more glorious than he is in this self-surrender. God is not more powerful than he is in this helplessness."[6]

God's strength is revealed in the weakness of the cross, God's wisdom in its foolishness. It is the way of the cross itself—the way of *kenosis,* lowering, losing—that leads to glory. We see here what Luther termed *absconditas sub contrario,* that is, truth which is "hidden under its opposite."[7] Jesus formulates his teachings as paradox (the greatest is the servant, the poor are blessed, lose your life to find it) in order to jar us out of our complacent thinking. Paul likewise deliberately speaks of the "foolishness" of the cross in the context of taking on the Corinthians' pride. That is, the intent is to unsettle the status quo of our thinking. Loving our enemies is counterintuitive because it cuts against the grain of our instincts, and therefore appears as foolishness and weakness, but in fact it is this way that is truly wise and truly powerful.

5. Luther, *Weimar Ausgabe,* 5.176.32–3. Emphasis in original.

6. Moltmann, *Crucified God,* 205. Moltmann's work here is based on his appropriation of Luther's *theologia crucis.* What Luther only sketched out in dramatic declarations, Moltmann has worked out into a nuanced theological proposal.

7. See McGrath, *Luther's Theology of the Cross,* esp. 148–75.

Now, none of this should be taken as a justification of suffering or subjection. Embracing paradox does not mean believing in the nonsensical or the abusive (that we should seek to suffer and die), rather it means jarring our thinking into a new counter-intuitive paradigm of enemy love which empowers and liberates us out of poverty, suffering, and domination structures. As Richard Hays writes,

> The image of the cross should not be used by those who hold power in order to ensure the acquiescent suffering of the powerless . . . The New Testament writers consistently employ the pattern of the cross precisely to call those who posses power and privilege to *surrender* it for the sake of the weak . . . In the New Testament's one clear application of this pattern to the patriarchal marriage relationship, it is husbands (not wives) who are called to emulate Christ's example of giving themselves up in obedience for the sake of the other (Eph 5:25) . . . It is precisely the focal image of the cross that ensures that the followers of Jesus—men and women alike—must read the New Testament as a call to renounce violence and coercion.[8]

The *theology of the cross*, properly understood, acts to subvert our "normal" way of thinking, flipping it on its head so it is conformed to the "upside-down" way of Jesus. It thus *crucifies* our normal conceptions of holiness, power, greatness, authority, justice, and glory. The theology of the cross means the death of all pride, triumphalism, judgment, and theologies of glory.

Because of this it is vital that *all our understandings of the atonement* be seen through the theology of the cross, which acts to reverse and subvert every metaphor and symbol: Christ, in ransoming us from the devil's bondage, does not condone the economy of slavery, but condemns it. The warfare imagery of victory in Christus Victor is likewise brought about through Christ's nonviolent submission, thus unmasking rather than glorifying violent conquest. Finally, in Christ taking our punishment, the legal system of retribution and revenge is not upheld, but condemned and overturned by grace (Rom 8:1–2). Each biblical metaphor here—economic, battlefield, and legal—can only be properly understood, not as affirmations of these systems, but as their subversion by grace.

---

8. Hays, *The Moral Vision of the New Testament*, 197. Emphasis in original.

God's hidden revelation	Revealed in its opposite
God's strength revealed	in the weakness of the cross
God's wisdom revealed	in the foolishness of the cross
Economy: Slavery overturned	by Christ paying a "ransom" to the devil
Battlefield: Unmasking violent conquest	via "victory" in Christus Victor
Legal: Retribution overturned by grace	by Christ taking our punishment

In all of this, it is crucial to remember that the theology of the cross is rooted in *paradox*. The theology of the cross is therefore not the glorification of death or abuse or suffering, but ultimately a theology focused on *life*, which seeks to end suffering, expose abuse, and overcome death.

A theology that glorifies suffering—as many forms of dour self-focused pietism have done over the centuries—is therefore a misrepresentation of the theology of the cross, and of the crucified one. Jesus does not call us to love suffering, but rather to love those who suffer, and consequently to live vulnerably in solidarity with them, in order to alleviate and end suffering by overcoming evil with grace. Sharing in the sufferings of Christ means joining him in radically loving others, especially the least. Its ultimate focus is on radically *loving*, not on suffering.[9]

The cross is indeed a shock, a scandal because it dares to face our suffering, mortality, and failure dead on. Yet right there at that point of loss and abandonment, in the agony of being godforsaken and accursed, as the skies above him turned black and the earth trembled, we see on that cross the truest picture of who God is. As we look on the horror and ugliness of the crucifixion we paradoxically see there on the cross the saving power and glory of God. God is there with us in the middle of abuse. God is there with us at our ugliest, and will not let anything estrange us or dehumanize us. God honors and loves us in that dehumanized state, and even refuses to dehumanize those who have dehumanized us.

The reason we focus on the cross is because of protest. We live in a broken world full of hurt, tragedy, and injustice. God is not triumphantly off in the clouds observing us from afar, God is here, among us in our pain. That is where we need to be too, close to those in need, close to the least. We focus on the cross to remember all of the victims around us, and to remember that—just as God was there when Jesus cried out in desperation on the cross, God is also there even in the middle of our pain and doubt.

9. For an extended treatment of this, see Hall, *The Cross in Our Context*.

A theology of the cross is a theology that identifies with the oppressed and the broken.

The cross is what we see now, but we know it is not the end. As we look on the horror and ugliness of the crucifixion we see there the God who is near, the God who suffers. Jesus reveals to us who God has always been. In Jesus we see that God has always suffered with those who suffer, God has always intimately known our condition, God has always been close to the broken-hearted. As Charles Dinsmore famously said over a century ago,

> There was a cross in the heart of God before there was one planted on the green hill outside Jerusalem. And now that the cross of wood has been taken down, the one in the heart of God abides.[10]

In that suffering God we meet the protesting God—a God who wants us to weep, who wants us to question, who wants us to resist.[11] The cry against injustice is one planted deep within the human soul. God has placed this cry in our hearts because God wants us to question suffering and injustice. Our Christian response to the questions of theodicy should not be to seek to find apologetic explanations, or to passively submit to suffering, but to join the protesting and suffering God in fighting to end human misery and injustice. A theology of the cross is a theology of protest. We focus on the cross in the hope that one day there will be no more crosses.

10. Dinsmore, *Atonement in Literature and Life*, 232.
11. See Moltmann, *Crucified God*, 48–53; 226–27.

10

A CRUCIFIED PEOPLE

Living the Theology of the Cross Through Love of Enemies

THE ATONEMENT IS INDEED vastly complex and hard for our minds to comprehend, but H.R. Mackintosh suggests that there is a still deeper reason that we do not understand the cross: Our real problem is not the lack of depth in our thinking, but the lack of depth in our character. In other words, our difficulty in comprehending the cross is not that our thoughts are not deep enough, but that our character is not. Our failure to understand is moral, not intellectual.

> We have never forgiven a deadly injury at a price like this, at such cost to ourselves as came upon God at Jesus' death. We fail to comprehend such sacrificial love because it far outstrips our shrunken conceptions of what love can endure. Let the man be found who has undergone the shattering experience of pardoning, nobly and tenderly, some awful wrong to himself, still more to one beloved by him, and he will understand the meaning of Calvary better than all the theologians in the world.[1]

Traditional understandings of the atonement have all too often produced theology that is divorced from the way and teachings of Jesus. The way of the cross *is* the way of Jesus, the way of enemy love. To miss this is to

---

1. Mackintosh, *The Christian Experience of Forgiveness*, 193.

fundamentally misunderstand the gospel. In fact, the vast majority of the New Testament's discussion of the atonement is not focused on *explaining* the atonement, but on extrapolating the implications of what it means for our relationship with God, and loving others based on what it reveals about God's true nature of Christ-likeness. We need to live out the cross to understand the cross. Our theories must provide for praxis. We really only learn what the atonement means when we learn to walk as Jesus did.

We are called away from the way of retribution, and towards the superior way of grace and enemy love, following God's example in Christ. Our way is the way of the cross, the way of self-sacrificing love that Jesus walked. This is a way that is directly opposed to the way of retribution. It does not retaliate, but proactively seeks to restore and redeem by bearing unjust suffering for the sake of love. The way embodied on the cross is not the way of violence, payback, and penalty, but the way of enemy love. When Paul implores us, like Christ, to become "living sacrifices" this is precisely the way he calls us to (Rom 12:1–21).

We learn who God truly is, and what the atonement means, as we learn to walk in the way of enemy love. As we take up our own cross, we will begin to glimpse what was going on in God's heart in choosing the cross. But as Mackintosh says, that kind of love is so hard to conceive because we have not found these depths in ourselves. It is through experiencing the depths of forgiveness for our own evil, and in learning what it means to forgive the very real hurt and betrayal done to us and those we love, that we truly begin to understand the cross and the depths of God's love. That is why Jesus declares that the prostitute who was washing his feet with her tears understood the heart of God more deeply than the Pharisees across the table from her, schooled in theology and the Bible.

It takes being broken by forgiveness to understand the cross. Without that, forgiveness seems to fly in the face of our natural understanding of justice. When I feel wronged I struggle with wanting payback. I smolder with self-righteous indignity. I feel I must defend my rights, not let any infraction go unpunished. Seeing this in myself, I understand how instinctual our need for retributive justice is, and why we are so drawn to it when we face injustice and pain. That is why basing our understanding of the atonement in the idea of payback justice is so dangerous—it is all too easy to focus on our own fleshly desire to condemn, and not on God's desire to show grace revealed in Christ. It is all too easy to become advocates of retribution, rather than advocates of God's radical way of the cross. Like

Peter, forbidding Christ to go to the cross (Matt 16:22), we think we are defending God's holiness and justice, when really we are standing opposed to God's costly way of grace revealed in Christ.

Love of enemies, admitting guilt, and forgiving wrongs are all acts that do not come naturally for us—neither on an individual nor international level. Yet it is precisely these acts of repentance and reconciliation that are so desperately needed in our world. Love of enemies is at once the most well-known teaching of Jesus, and the least practiced. As G.K. Chesterton famously said, the way of Jesus has not been tried and found lacking, it has been found difficult and not tried.[2] I say that to myself as much as to anyone else. I acknowledge my own pride and unwillingness to forgive, my own need to follow better in the way of the cross. But regardless of how difficult, foreign, or painful the way of the cross is, it is the way Jesus calls us to.

A CHANGE OF PERSPECTIVE

C.S. Lewis once commented that he found the distinction of "loving the sinner but hating the sin" to be absurd. How can you separate the two? How can you hate what someone *does*, but not hate *them*? Until it occurred to him that there was one man who he had been doing this with his entire life—himself.[3] Loving our enemies simply means loving others the way we love ourselves. It is summed up in Christ's teaching to "do unto others as you would have them do unto you" (Luke 6:31). Treating others as we would want to be treated, and desiring the best for them.

This entails a change in perspective: we normally define ourselves by the various social groups we identify with. Our family, our friends, our country, our ethnic group, our religion, all constitute how we define who *we* are. Loving our enemies is the radical widening of this definition of "we" to include even those we would seek to exclude. It breaks the "us versus them" divide and joins Christ who "has made the two groups one and has destroyed the barrier, the dividing wall of hostility" (Eph 2:14). The enemy, the outsider, the other is therefore shown grace, with the goal being the restoration of relationship.

This focus on relationship is crucial. Forgiveness is often understood in individualistic terms: Ministers speak of receiving forgiveness so we can be released from guilt. Therapists speak of forgiving another so we can be

2. Chesterton, *What's Wrong With The World*, 29.
3. Quoted in Yancey, *What's so Amazing about Grace?*, 280.

healed of the wounds of our past. These are true and important aspects of forgiveness as far as they go, but at its core forgiveness is not only about restoring us as individuals, it is about restoring *relationship* with others. Even when we think of forgiveness in a strictly vertical dimension, forgiveness is not primarily about our absolution or assurance, it is about restoring our relationship with God. That restored relationship with God is meant to carry over into restored relationships with others, as we learn to love others as God has loved us.

Our very identity as humans is found in relationship. As babies we begin life as self-focused and gradually learn to see ourselves as beings in relationship as we learn to love and be loved. That relational love from our parents shapes our self-image, who we are. Growing into maturity entails progressing from the individual-self to the social-self. In other words, in developing empathy, learning to love others as we love ourselves. Forgiving and being forgiven is vital to our well-being precisely because we are social and relational beings. To shut out forgiveness (both being forgiven and showing forgiveness) is to shut out love.

Now, forgiveness does not mean simply saying "that's okay." If it were okay, there would be nothing to forgive. What it does mean is that our response (towards ourselves, and towards the other who has wronged us) is in the interest of love. That is of course easier said than done because when we are wronged our instinct is not to love the other, but to "make them pay." Love of enemies is about moving out of an "us versus them" perspective to seeing that there is only "us." *We* should care for each other, but *we* do things that are hurtful, sinful, and evil. So forgiveness seeks to open the doors for *our* restitution (both restoring the one who was wronged, and the wrong-doer). It asks: What can I do to break us both out of the trap of hostility?

Forgiveness means being willing to allow God to use us as an instrument of love for that person, opening the door for the possibility of reconciliation and redemption. It does not ignore or condone sin, but rather involves honestly facing the real hurt done to us, as well as facing the blame we also bear, and pro-actively working towards mending this, beginning in our own hearts. Again, our model for this kind of love is God in Christ, who did not condone or ignore our sin, but instead acted in love to break us out of sin's bondage—not demanding payback, but giving his very life for us on the cross. We truly understand what the cross means by walking in the way of the cross, by radically loving and being loved.

OVERCOMING EVIL WITH GOOD

Love of enemies begins with a healthy self-love and then expands our perspective from a *me*-focus to a *we*-focus. It breaks us out of destructive us versus them thinking, and instead tells us to treat our adversary with the same love that we would wish for ourselves. But how do we break out of the cycle of hurting and being hurt? Hatred breeds hatred. Retaliation escalates to more retaliation. We hate people who hate, and in so doing become what we hate. When we feel accused we seek to condemn back. When there is a spirit of fear, panic becomes contagious.

We break that cycle of hurt by *acting in the opposite spirit*, thus shifting the course of the seemingly inevitable spiral of escalation. Paul calls us to not be overcome by evil, but to "overcome evil with good" (Rom 12:21). This idea of responding in the opposite spirit is expressed beautifully in the famous prayer of St Francis of Assisi,

> Lord, make me an instrument of Thy peace
> where there is hatred, let me sow love
> where there is injury, pardon
> where there is doubt, faith
> where there is despair, hope
> where there is darkness, light
> and where there is sadness, joy.

What makes this particularly difficult is that love goes against the grain of our thinking when we are in the middle of conflict. In the heat of conflict our minds become clouded with pride and pain. Because we feel threatened, our primary goal becomes self-preservation at the expense of a relational orientation. We therefore need to begin imagining positive ways we can respond in the spirit of enemy love, *before* we find ourselves in the heat of conflict.

In general, love of enemies involves widening our perspective, and works through the principle of overcoming evil with good. Within that basic definition, however, there are a virtually unlimited number of creative ways to apply these principles in our lives. Jesus describes several different scenarios of loving our enemies: turning the other cheek, walking the extra mile, and giving the shirt off your back (Matt 5:39–41). This variety of examples indicates that applying love of enemies requires vigorous creativity to imagine how it can be applied in different situations.

Allow me a brief excursion of what such creativity might look like on the topic of international conflict and war. On both sides of this debate are people who deeply care about people's welfare: On the one hand, we have those who say it would be immoral to simply stand by when others are being attacked. We need to defend our families, our homes. If we care about people, and want to avoid bloodshed, then a policy of "turning the other cheek" seems irresponsible if that means a country should do nothing when its people are being killed. Pacifism should not mean passivity. On the other hand, we have those who have seen the devastation of war. They have seen violence spiral into an endless cycle of retaliation, and they just want it to stop.

The question then becomes: how can we address both of these legitimate concerns? How can we protect life, and reverse the dynamics of violence rather than participating in it? What are steps we can *actively* take to reduce violence in our world? In other words, rather than debating whether or not it is ever acceptable to participate in violence (where the only two choices seem to be either bloodshed or inaction) perhaps what we need to be asking instead is *what can we do to reduce violence?*[4]

The answers to these questions will of course be complex and varied. They will require techniques of diplomacy, conflict resolution, social reform, and nonviolent action, just to name a few. One major factor in reducing violence involves reducing injustice in our world. Reducing poverty and promoting human rights are of course immensely complex problems in their own right. And this is only the topic of war. We have not even addressed how this might affect how we approach the issues of domestic violence or crime. How can we better address and care for the needs of those who have been violated by crime? How can we make our homes and neighborhoods safer? How can we work towards real reform among criminals so that they become morally responsible and compassionate?[5]

These are the kinds of questions a focus on restorative justice asks. It goes without saying, however, that there is no one-size-fits-all solution to the many problems and conflicts we face. It will require lots of work and lots of intelligence and creativity. But the place to start is to break out of the stalemate between the false choices of violence or inaction, and instead ask how we, in each particular situation, can act to overcome evil and hurt with love.

---

4. For some concrete proposals for reducing violence and dealing with international conflict, see Stassen, *Just Peacemaking.*

5. For a detailed treatment of this see Zehr, *Changing Lenses.*

Our model for this kind of enemy love is found at the cross. God shows us how to love by loving us while we were enemies. The teachings of Jesus were important because they served as commentary on Christ's saving actions, but the real focus of the Gospels is on what Jesus did—caring for the poor, healing the sick, loving the condemned—all culminating at the cross were his action of loving us while we where his enemies resulted in our salvation and reconciliation. In the same way, we proclaim that Gospel not only with words, but much more in how we *exhibit* the way of Jesus by loving our enemies, by demonstrating grace. If Jesus is truly Lord of all, then we need to exhibit love of enemies in every aspect of society.

THE MYTH OF INNOCENCE

The hardest part, however, is not the complexity of these problems, but the polarized us versus them perspective that keeps us from truly seeing the other, and loving them as we love ourselves. We all have been hurt, but none of us wants to own up to hurting others. For some reason we can easily see the most trivial speck or flaw in others, while being oblivious to the most glaring faults and hypocrisy in our own lives. Loving our enemies is about reversing that imbalance in our vision. It means both seeing the other with the same mercy we would wish for ourselves, and simultaneously recognizing that what we most hate in others is often a reflection of what we hate in ourselves. We project these judgments outwards onto others because it is too threatening to direct them towards ourselves.

When my daughter was four years old she carelessly hit me in the face with a stick. I managed to suppress my instinct to scream, and silently held my hands to my face, cowering in pain. That silence was too much for my little girl to bear, and she burst into tears, saying, "I'm mad at you, because you're making me feel bad!" These were not tears of sympathy for me, they were tears of anger at how her own guilt made her feel, directed towards me. Still in pain—and understandably still feeling anger more than I did compassion—I found myself in the position of needing to hug and console her, rather than being consoled. She was at the time so focused on herself that she was incapable of recognizing how her actions had hurt me. It was more than she could bear.

Guilt is threatening. We feel accused, attacked, and respond either by defending ourselves or by throwing back accusations. That is the perspective little children like my daughter naturally have, and whenever I feel wronged or triggered I find myself instantly reverting back into that self-focused childish perspective as well. It is all too easy from that perspective to marshal a host of noble moral and religious arguments as to why it is "right" and "just" to feel this way. This is something we can observe in the language of those who advocate retributive justice, but behind this lofty language is a core instinct, a primal emotion that we all know from childhood that is rooted in self-focus.

No one needs to teach a child things like "that's mine" and "he hit me first so I can hit him back" but children *do* need to be taught empathy. Retribution is instinctual, compassion is learned. There is a huge emotional pull in us towards payback justice, but we need to realize that this is ultimately preschool morality. What we need is a change in perspective, moving from a *me*-orientation to a *we*-orientation. Conscience is awakened in us when we recognize the results our sin has on others. In other words, being shown compassion leads to us having compassion towards others. People who know their own need for mercy in turn show mercy to others. This kind of empathy is not our nature, it is learned in relationship. We learn to love and have empathy by being loved and shown empathy.

When I first came to Christ I was hardly aware of how much I needed mercy and forgiveness. Surrounded in a dark world I could not see my own shadow. The closer I moved to Christ, the more the bright light of his love caused the shadows I cast to deepen their contours. So now years later I am finally coming to realize more than ever how deeply I need to show others the same mercy I so desperately need—a mercy I received before I even knew to ask. In particular, my sinfulness is most revealed in my seeming inability to forgive and show mercy when I feel wronged. I need to own up to that ugliness in myself and say "I do want to love my enemies, Lord, help my lovelessness. Have mercy on me, a sinner."

THE DEPTH OF PAIN

At the outset of this chapter we read the statement of H.R. Mackintosh that the only way for us to truly grasp the depths of God's love for us on the cross is by experiencing and practicing that same love in our own lives. As Mackintosh said, "Let the man be found who has undergone the shattering experience of pardoning, nobly and tenderly, some awful wrong to himself, still more to one beloved by him, and he will understand the meaning of

Calvary better than all the theologians in the world."[6] I would like to share the story of a man like that.

In *A Grace Disguised*, Gerald Sittser tells how his mother, wife, and daughter were all killed in a car crash by a drunk driver. The kind of loss that Sittser endured is devastating, and the rage, disbelief, and pain one feels are normal and healthy ways of dealing with such crushing loss. The process of forgiving someone for a wrong in many ways dovetails with the process of grieving and loss. The anger we feel is just as real and legitimate an emotion as our grief. The problem is when we get stuck in that anger, re-living it again and again on the canvas of our minds, instead of facing the loss and allowing life to go on and ourselves to heal. Sittser writes of how he dealt with that grief and anger together with his surviving children.

> It was the brokenness of my children that reminded me every day that they had had their fill of suffering. I did not want to see them suffer anymore. I realized that my unforgiveness would only prolong their pain. I knew that they were watching me, whether deliberately or unknowingly, to see how I responded to the wrong done to us. If I was unforgiving, they would most likely be unforgiving. If I was obsessed with the wrong done to me, they would be too . . . I did not want such a plague in my home. I did not want to raise bitter children. So I chose to forgive, for their sake as well as my own.[7]

Sittser describes the stages of grief—*denial, anger, bargaining, depression*, and (he adds) *binging*—not as phases that he had to go through once, but as feelings and temptations he had to continually deal with which all masked the real blackness and loss he finally had to face beneath them all. He says that he will never "get over" the loss of three generations of his family, and does not even want to, but tells how he was able to find *a grace disguised* in his pain, a way to let the darkness transform rather than destroy, to let loss enlarge the soul rather than crush it.

> Recovery is a misleading and empty expectation. We recover from broken limbs, not amputations. Catastrophic loss by definition precludes recovery. It will transform us or destroy us, but we will never be the same. There is no going back to the past which is gone forever, only going ahead . . . Whatever the future is, it will, and must, contain the pain of the past with it. Sorrow

6. Mackintosh, 193.

7. Sittser, *A Grace Disguised*, 26.

never entirely leaves the soul of those who have suffered a severe loss . . . this depth of sorrow is the sign of a healthy soul . . . it enlarges the soul until the soul is capable of mourning and rejoicing simultaneously, of feeling the world's pain and hoping for the world's healing at the same time.[8]

Pain and loss can enter into our lives in many ways. Through illness or an accident, through our being wronged by another, or by our own brokenness and folly. With any type of loss, it is not so important what has happened as it is how we deal with it. In the same way that the shame, betrayal, and forsakenness of the Cross led to Christ's resurrection and our redemption, loss has the potential to deepen us, to open our eyes to how precious every moment of life is, showing us meaning in the darkness.

This experience of allowing pain to enlarge our souls has been the tale told out of the most profound depths of human misery. Viktor Frankl, a psychologist and survivor of the Nazi death camps, speaks of how he saw that blackness of night bring out both the best and worst in the human soul. From that experience he went on to ground an entire branch of psychology on nurturing the human capacity to find meaning, even in the very pit of darkness.[9] Similarly Aleksandr Solzhenitsyn writes of how in the dehumanizing Gulag of Stalin's Russia he was able to transcend death and find life, so that he could say to the astonishment of those around him, "bless you, prison, for having been in my life."[10]

THE IMITATION OF CHRIST

Solzhenitsyn endured the Gulag, Frankl the Holocaust, and Sittser the loss of three generations in an instant. In the face of enduring such catastrophic suffering and loss we may be tempted to see such people as somehow "super human," but suffering is common to all of our lives. What their stories show us is a possibility in our suffering to find a depth to life that we did not know existed before. All of us face, on big and small scales, very real pain, loss, and evil in our lives. Into every one of our lives, there comes a cross. Whether it is losing a loved one to terminal illness, the pain of divorce, or facing our own brokenness and failings, we all experience darkness and suffering in our lives. As we love others, we open ourselves up to sharing in theirs.

8. Ibid., 62–63

9. Frankl, *Man's Search for Meaning*.

10. Solzhenitsyn, *The Gulag Archipelago*, 313

Regardless of the cause of our suffering—whether we are enduring hardship standing up for love, we have been wronged and betrayed by someone we had trusted, or tragedy has unexpectedly struck our lives—we can go through that darkness together with Christ. Our pain can become a means of redemption. On the cross God in Christ entered into our brokenness and sorrow, and that is where we find God now. In the darkness, God is there. That does not mean that when we face trouble and loss it is somehow painless. God is there in the darkness, but that darkness is real. Sittser writes,

> When we plunge into darkness, it is darkness we experience. We feel pain, anguish, sorrow, and despair, and we experience the ugliness, meaninglessness, and absurdity of life. We brood as well as hope, rage as well as surrender, doubt as well as believe. We are apathetic as often as we are hopeful, and sorrowful before we are joyful.[11]

Facing our own darkness is hard, and it is hard to be close to those who are suffering, but as we face our own pain and weakness we become more sensitive to the pain and need of others. When we love others, sharing in their pain, the New Testament tells us something incredible happens: when we suffer for the sake of love we "share in the sufferings of Christ" (1 Pet 4:12–13, cf. Rom 8:17; 2 Thess 1:5). Like Simon of Cyrene we can share the awesome privilege of lifting the cross off of the shoulders of Christ, and carry the burdens of God with him.

We should not seek suffering, we should seek to end it. But there will be times, when standing up for what is right, where suffering will be unavoidable. In Christ we see that God is close to all who are grieving and burdened. God is with us in all of our suffering. Scripture shows that there is a special solidarity that Jesus has with us when we take up the same cross that our Lord carried, when we suffer for the sake of the least, when we endure hardship standing up for love. It is in these times that we can in our darkness participate in "the fellowship of sharing in his sufferings" (Phil 3:10).

This does not mean that suffering is somehow glorified. Evil remains evil no matter how much good comes out of it. Romans 8:28 does not say that God "makes all things good," but that "in all things God works for the good." Despite the injustice and agony of the cross, God used it to bring

11. Sittser, 40.

about life. God can do the same with the crosses in our own lives as we take on suffering for the sake of others.

APPENDIX

Three Greek Word Studies on God's Justice and Justification in Romans

IN CHAPTER 2 WE read N.T Wright's declaration that Paul's term *dikaiosynē theou* in Romans 3:21 refers not only to God's justice, but specifically to God's act of *restorative* justice. As Wright says, it is "the instrument of putting the world to rights—what we might call cosmic restorative justice."[1] Wright employs two interconnected concepts here: first the overall framework of God's action in Jesus—the *dikaiosynē theou*, understood as God's act of restorative justice. Second, the vehicle of this restorative action: justification, which he describes in terms of God "putting to rights" us and our broken world.

In this appendix we take a deeper look at the exegetical evidence behind the understandings of these two ideas, beginning with Paul's understanding of the *dikaiosynē theou* in this first section. Following that, we will explore Paul's concept of justification—understood within this restorative context not merely as a legal declaration, but as an act of God that is transforming and life-giving. Finally, in the third and final section, we will look at the much debated term *hilastērion* in Romans 3:25, and how the restorative context of Romans 3:21–26 sheds light on how we understand the atonement as an act of healing rather than appeasement.

---

1. Wright, "Letter to the Romans," 400.

Appendix

THE RIGHTEOUSNESS/JUSTICE OF GOD

The Greek word *dikaiosynē* can be translated as either righteousness or justice. An example of this can be found in this very passage where the NIV first translates *dikaiosynē* as "righteousness" and then shifts to translating it as "justice"

> But now a *righteousness (dikaiosynē)* from God, apart from law, has been made known, to which the Law and the Prophets testify. This *righteousness (dikaiosynē)* from God comes through faith in Jesus Christ to all who believe . . . He did this to demonstrate his *justice (dikaiosynē)*, because in his forbearance he had left the sins committed beforehand unpunished. (Rom 3:21–25)

It is important to note that *dikaiosynē* refers to justice specifically in the sense of doing what is *just* and *good*. That's why the word is almost always translated as "righteousness" in order to indicate that sense. *Dikaiosynē* is the same word the LXX[2] uses to translate the Hebrew word *tsedaqah* in the Old Testament. Now, there are several words for justice in Hebrew. *Tsedaqah* in particular is almost always translated as "righteousness" in the Old Testament because of its connection with the character of God. Paul's conception of justice was very likely shaped by this Hebrew concept of justice, rooted in the idea of God's goodness. That is, *dikaiosynē* does not mean justice in the sense of impartiality, but in the sense of *doing what is good and right*.

What Paul is describing here is the demonstration of God's *justice*, against the claim that God acted unjustly in not punishing sin. More specifically, he is describing a *righteousness* that comes from God which makes us righteous. In other words, it is God's act of setting things right, of making good. Paul therefore opens this passage by declaring that now, in Christ, God's (restorative) justice has been revealed, *apart from* the law. In other words, he juxtaposes God's restorative justice—the "righteousness/justice *from* God"—over against the law's system of reward and punishment, blessings and curses. He is contrasting the idea of God's restorative justice with the law's principle of retributive justice.

Being rooted in retributive justice "the law brings wrath" (Rom 4:15), and therefore only serves the function of exposing sin (Rom 3:20). The law

---

2. The LXX is the Greek translation of the Old Testament used by the authors of the New Testament.

is itself powerless to save us because it is unable to "impart life" (Gal 3:21).[3] That is, Paul's central critique of the law is that it is not *restorative*, not *life-giving*. This restoration, Paul declares, can only come through the indwelling of the Spirit, received by faith, not law (Gal 3:2). We are therefore "not under the law, but under grace" (Rom 6:14), meaning we are no longer under the law of retributive justice and wrath (which brings death), but under Christ's law of restorative justice and redemption (which brings salvation, life, and regeneration). "Therefore, there is now no condemnation," there is no retribution, "because through Christ Jesus the law of the Spirit who gives life," that is, God's *life-imparting* restorative action, "has set you free from the law of sin and death," set us free from the law of retributive justice (Rom 8:1–3).

Now, while Paul juxtaposes the law's retributive justice with God's restorative justice, in this same sentence he immediately asserts that God's restorative justice, this "righteousness from/of God," is "testified to in the law and prophets." In other words, while the New Testament contains a major critique of the law, a critique of the way of punitive justice, it at the same time maintains that the message of grace is woven throughout all of Scripture. Indeed, as Paul says, we do in fact find that very idea of restorative justice in the law and prophets. Notice how in the following passages justice and mercy are not in conflict, but rather *doing justice* means performing acts of mercy[4]:

> Learn to do right! *Seek justice*: Defend the oppressed. Take up the cause of the fatherless, plead the case of the widow (Isa 1:17).

> *Administer justice* every morning; rescue from the hand of his oppressor the one who has been robbed (Jer 21:12).

The way that we "administer justice," the prophets tell us, is by encouraging and helping the oppressed. God's justice is not in conflict with God's mercy, they are inseparable. What Zechariah calls "true justice" can only come *through* mercy:

---

3. The Greek word here is *zōopoiēsai* which means "to make alive." Compare this to Rom 5:18 where Paul speaks of how the work of Christ "resulted in justification and life" and 5:21 where he refers to "righteousness to bring eternal life."

4. In the following passages I have added italics and modified the punctuation from the NIV. The original Hebrew of course has no italics and no punctuation, so punctuation is always interpretive.

> This is what the LORD Almighty said: "*Administer true justice: show mercy and compassion to one another*" (Zech 7:9).

> "Yet the LORD longs to be gracious to you; therefore he will rise up to show you compassion. *For the LORD is a God of justice*" (Isa 30:18).

If we want to understand justice as the prophets did, then we need to understand justice in terms of *setting things right again*.

JUSTIFICATION MEANS MAKING-RIGHT

Along with *dikaiosynē*, another critical word in Romans 3:21–26 is the related term *dikaioō*, which is commonly translated in English as "justified."[5] Paul writes, "all have sinned and fall short of the glory of God, and are *justified* (*dikaioō*) freely by his grace through the redemption that came by Christ Jesus" (vv. 23–24). The word *dikaioō* here is usually taken to mean "declare righteous" or "vindicate."

This reading would coincide with its common usage in the Greek version of the Old Testament (the LXX), where it clearly refers to making correct deliberations—to *recognizing* someone's goodness as in a judicial pronouncement.[6] However, this is not the way Paul is using the term here. This becomes quite clear when we look at the next chapter of Romans where Paul declares that "God *justifies* (*dikaioō*) the ungodly" (Rom 4:5). Here Paul makes a shocking statement that seems to blatantly contradict the Old Testament prohibition on justifying the ungodly. Take a look at these passages from the LXX, and notice how we find the *exact same Greek wording* as we do in Romans 4:5, yet in these Old Testament passages it is expressly condemned:

> **Isa 5:23:** They *justify the ungodly* (*dikaiounta ton asebē*) for the sake of bribes and take away the rights of the righteous.[7]

---

5. Both the verb *dikaioō* and the related noun *dikaiosynē* come from the same Greek root *dik* in the same way that the verb justify and the noun justice are related in English.

6. See for example Deut 25:1; 1 Kgs 8:32, Isa 43:9, Job 33:32, Gen 44:16, Isa 43:26, Ps 51:4 (=LXX 50:6).

7. Author's translation from the LXX.

Exod 23:7: Keep away from unjust sentences, you shall not execute the innocent and righteous, and you shall not *justify the ungodly* (*dikaiounta ton asebē*) for the sake of bribes.[8]

Rom 4:5: But to one who without works trusts him who *justifies the ungodly* (*dikaiounta ton asebē*), such faith is reckoned as righteousness. (NRSV)

The Hebrew of Exodus 23:7 makes this contrast even more pronounced. There God boldly declares, "I will not justify the ungodly," in sharp contrast to Paul's statement. Citing the above verses, James Dunn writes, "To justify the ungodly or acquit the wicked was abhorrent to a basic and frequently repeated canon of Jewish justice."[9]

So if that's true, how can Paul claim that God justifies the ungodly when his Bible seems to expressly forbid this? The problem comes from translating *dikaioō* as "declare righteous" in Romans. Again, this is clearly the sense of the word in Isaiah and Exodus above (where it is condemned!), but unless we want to suppose that Paul is contradicting Scripture, this cannot be what he means in Romans.

The answer, I would propose, is that Paul is using *dikaioō* in a different sense, which entails more than a mere legal acquittal, more that declaring someone to be innocent after receiving a payment. While *dikaioō* can mean "declare righteous," it can also mean "make pure" and "set free."[10] An example of this can be seen in Paul's statement that we have been "co-crucified" with Christ so that we would "no longer be slaves to sin—because anyone who has died has been *set free* (*dikaioō*) from sin" (Rom 6:6–7).

Even where *dikaioō* appears to mean "declare righteous" linguistically in Romans, I would argue that it nevertheless always includes the *restorative* sense of God *making-righteous* the unrighteous in Paul's thought. We can see this connection explicitly drawn out in Romans 5 where Paul juxtaposes two parallel formulations:

---

8. Author's translation.

9. Dunn, *Romans*, 204.

10. An example of *dikaioō* meaning "make pure" can be found in Ps 73:13 (=LXX 72:13) where David complains "in vain I have kept my heart *pure*." Here the Hebrew word *zakah* meaning "pure" is translated in the LXX with the Greek *dikaioō*. Similarly, the Hebrew word *tsadaq*, which is the word usually translated with *dikaioō* in the LXX, can also mean "purify." An example is Daniel speaking of the temple being "made *tsadaq*" (Dan 8:14), which various English translations have interpreted to mean "cleansed" (KJV, ASV), "restored" (NRSV, NLT), or "reconsecrated" (NIV).

Consequently, just as one trespass resulted in condemnation for all people,	For just as through the disobedience of the one man the many were made sinners,
so also one righteous act resulted in *justification* (*dikaiōsis*[11]) and life for all people. (v. 18)	so also through the obedience of the one man the many will be *made righteous*. (v. 19)

Here we can see that, whatever Paul understands *dikaioō* to mean, he directly connotes that meaning with our being "made righteous" in this parallel verse. The NET renders the Greek *dikaiōsin zōēs* (literally "the making-right of/from life") as "righteousness leading to life" (v. 18). Justification is an act of God that results in life because it "makes righteous."

When Paul says that "God justifies the ungodly," he is not proposing the God is a participant in the kind of legal fiction that the Old Testament expressly condemns. Indeed, one of Paul's central points in Romans is to demonstrate that God was not unjust in showing mercy to sinners rather than punishing them. The way that God demonstrates justice is not by acquitting the unrighteous, but by making them good. It is a gospel of God's act of restorative justice in us. God's actions are life-giving and transforming.

Therefore, if we wish to translate *dikaioō* as "declared righteous," we must always remember that for Paul this entails our being *made righteous* as a consequence. Perhaps we might think of it as similar to how God *spoke* in Genesis, and life was created. As James Denney wrote, more than a century ago, "The paradoxical phrase, Him that justifieth the ungodly, does not suggest that justification is a fiction, whether legal or any other sort, but that it is a miracle. It is a thing that only God can achieve."[12]

As Paul says, no human being will be *recognized as righteous* (*dikaioō*) before God by observance of the law (Rom 3:20), but we can be *made righteous* by God's life-giving righteousness. When *dikaioō* is read in this way, what Paul writes in Romans 4:5 is no longer a contradiction to what we read in the law (Exod 23:7) and the prophets (Isa 5:23), but its *solution*:

> But to one who without works trusts him who *makes the ungodly righteous/pure*, such faith is reckoned as righteousness (Rom 4:5).

Any lingering doubts of this interpretation of *dikaioō* are removed when we read Paul's declaration that God has made Jesus "to be sin who

11. *Dikaiōsis* is the noun form of the verb *dikaioō*

12. James Denney, "Paul's Epistle to the Romans," 616.

knew no sin, so that in him *we might become the righteousness of God*" (2 Cor 5:21, NRSV). Let me repeat that again: We become the *dikaiosynē theou*. God's righteousness causes us to *become* God's righteousness. Again, this is justification in the sense of being relationally *set right*, entailing real change in who we are, and how we live and think, effected in us by the indwelling life of God. In other words, our experience of the indwelling Spirit in a loving relationship transforms us into Christ-likeness. That is what justification means. It is a restorative, life-imparting act. Paul's understanding of the cross is within the context of restoration and healing, not punishment and appeasement.

PROPITIATION COMES THROUGH EXPIATION

This context of God's restorative and life-imparting justice "making right" the ungodly gives us insight into the much debated term *hilastērion* in Romans 3:25. Paul writes there that God presented Christ as a *hilastērion* through trust in his blood. Proponents of penal substitution want to translate *hilastērion* as "propitiation," from the verb "propitiate" meaning "to make favorable," implying that the atonement is about turning aside wrath through appeasement. Many others have argued that it should instead be translated as expiation, meaning the removal or "covering" of sin, implying that the atonement is about purification and cleansing. The classic argument here is exemplified by the debate between C.H Dodd and Leon Morris. John Stott sums up Dodd's argument regarding the *hilaskomai* word group as follows:

> [Dodd] argued that in the LXX the word *kipper* (the Hebrew word for "atone") was sometimes translated by Greek words other than *hilaskomai*, which mean to "purify" or "cancel"; that *hilaskomai* in the LXX sometimes translates other Hebrew words than *kipper*, which mean to "cleanse" and "forgive"; and that when *hilaskomai* does translate *kipper* the meaning is expiation or the removal of defilement.[13]

While Morris agrees with Dodd on several points (in particular that one should not see propitiation in terms of the "pagan sense of a crude propitiation of an angry deity"), he nevertheless argues that, because Paul

13. Stott, *Cross of Christ*, 170.

opens Romans with the problem of God's wrath, the solution he provides here must involve the turning away of wrath.[14]

While it is true enough that Christ's atonement addresses the problem of wrath, what this misses is the *means* by which God's wrath is averted in Paul's argument. Wrath is averted (propitiated) because God *removes* our sin (expiation) in the act of *making us right*. This is the whole point of the *dikaiosynē theou*—God's action to make right sinful humanity—which is Paul's central point here. Reading *hilastērion* as "expiation" therefore makes sense contextually within Paul's current argument, whereas reading it as "propitiation" (or "mercy seat" for that matter) turns it into a non sequitur. It is not the appeasement of God's wrath that allows God to forgive; it is the healing of our sin-stained hearts that removes the *cause* of God's righteous anger.[15] Morris suggests this himself when he proposes that "forgiveness or purging of sin is one which involves, as a necessary feature, the putting away of the divine wrath."[16] Wrath is turned away by the purging of sin. Our problem, then, is not God's willingness to love and forgive us, but the objective reality of our brokenness being in need of a real cure. God is just in not punishing because true justice comes about by *making us* just and good.

It would be good at this point to say a few words about how we are to understand the idea of "wrath" here. Language of God's wrath or anger was common at the time of the Bible. Similar to the idea of God's "jealousy," the idea of God's "anger" was used by the prophets to convey God's passion for humanity, and utter opposition to oppression and injustice. Such anthropomorphism expressed that God cared deeply about people. Nevertheless, it is a concept that is deeply problematic for modern readers. This is because speaking of God's "anger" draws the focus away from our sin, and instead places it on God's feelings, as if the problem was with God rather than us. The image of violent punishment is understandably associated by many people today with abuse rather than justice. Because of this, the image of

---

14. Morris, *Apostolic Preaching*, 173.

15. As James Dunn notes, translating *hilastērion* as "propitiation" is problematic since God is the one who provides the *hilastērion*, and one logically cannot appease oneself. Similarly, Dunn notes that in Old Testament usage God is never the object of the parallel Hebrew term *kipper*. "Properly speaking, in the Israelite cult, God is never 'propitiated' or 'appeased.' The objective of the atoning act is rather the removal of sin—that is, either by purifying the person or object or wiping out the sin. . . . [T]he atoning act thus removes the sin which provoked God's wrath, but it does so by acting on the sin, rather than acting on God" (Dunn, *Theology of Paul*, 214).

16. Morris, *Apostolic Preaching*, 157.

God's wrath does not connote a picture of justice, but instead conveys a picture of injustice and hurt.

It was clearly not the intent of the biblical writers to portray God as unjust and immoral, so we need to seriously question whether this is the best language with which to convey these concepts to people today. If the picture of God's wrath draws our attention to God's emotions—evoking a picture of self-focused immaturity, rather than of compassionate righteousness—then perhaps we need to take another look at what we are saying.

Because of this, I believe it is more helpful today to think of wrath in terms of the impersonal consequence of sin, rather than in terms of God's anger. Doing so stresses that what we are dealing with is the inevitable consequence for an action. It follows from sin like falling is the consequence of jumping off a cliff. This is a move we can already see Paul moving towards himself: When Paul speaks of wrath, he moves away from the Old Testament images of God's emotional anger, and towards a conception of wrath focused on *natural consequence*.[17] He writes in Romans that "the wages of sin is death" (Rom 6:23). A wage is the *result* or *consequence* of working. Paul similarly speaks of *inheriting* either destruction or life, and of the *fruits* of our actions. All of these convey the idea of *natural consequence*, reaping what we sow. In Romans 1:18-32, the longest discourse on wrath in the New Testament, Paul retains the language of "wrath" from the Old Testament, but now speaks of us being *given over* to sinful desires (1:24), shameful lusts (1:26), and a depraved mind (1:28). In this way, Paul says, people "received in themselves the due penalty for their error" (1:27). That is, Paul describes how God's wrath consists in leaving us to the consequence of our actions, rather than in God actively punishing us. The "punishment" is for God to step away and let us do what we want.

In one sense we could think of this as the just consequence of hurtful behavior. God leaves us to our own devices, and we reap destruction. At the same time, in both the Old and New Testaments wrath is always spoken of with an accompanying plea for repentance, for people not to go towards self-destruction. In the Gospels we see this in connection with Jesus' plea for people to turn away from the cycle of violence associated with the way of retaliation, urging them instead to embrace the way of grace and enemy love. It is the enemy love of God that acts to break us out of the treadmill of death, the vicious circle of hurting and being hurt. So while these spiraling consequences of hurt can in one sense be understood as "just deserts,"

---

17. For a comprehensive study, see Hanson, *The Wrath of the Lamb.*

they are not God's ultimate desire, which is to see us liberated from these treadmills of death.

BIBLIOGRAPHY

Arbesmann, Rudolph. "The Concept of 'Christus Medicus' in St. Augustine." *Traditio*, vol. 10 (1954), 1–28.

Athanasius. *On the Incarnation of the Word*. In *Nicene and Post Nicene Fathers, Second Series*, vol. 4. Edited by Philip Schaff and Henry Wace, 31–67. Grand Rapids: Eerdmans, 1952.

Augustine. *Contra Faustum*. In *Nicene and Post Nicene Fathers, First Series*, vol. 4. Edited by Philip Schaff, 155–345. Peabody, MA: Hendrickson, 1999.

———. "Exposition on the Psalms." In *Nicene and Post Nicene Fathers, First Series*, vol. 8. Edited by Philip Schaff, 189–97. Peabody, MA: Hendrickson, 1999.

———. "On Nature and Grace." In *The Works of St Augustine—A Translation for the 21st Century*, vol. 1/23. Edited by John E. Rotelle, 225–70. New York: New City, 1990.

Aulén, Gustav. *Christus Victor—An Historical Study of the Three Main Types of the Idea of the Atonement*. New York: Macmillan, 1977.

Bondi, Roberta C. *Memories of God: Theological Reflections on a Life*. Nashville: Abingdon, 1995.

Boyd, Gregory. *God at War: The Bible and Spiritual Conflict*. Downers Grove, IL: Intervarsity, 1997.

Brueggemann, Walter. *Westminster Bible Companion: Isaiah 40–66*. Louisville: Westminster John Knox, 1998.

———. *Theology of the Old Testament*. Minneapolis: Fortress, 1997.

Calvin, John. *Institutes of the Christian Religion*. Grand Rapids: Eerdmans, 1957.

Carroll, John T. "Sickness and Healing in the New Testament Gospels." *Interpretation* 49.2 (April 1995), 130–42.

Chesterton, Gilbert Keith. *What's Wrong with the World*. Mineola, NY: Dover, 2007.

Denney, James. "St. Paul's Epistle to the Romans." In *Expositors Greek Testament*. Edited by W. Robertson Nicoll. London: Hodder & Stoughton, 1897.

Dinsmore, Charles. *Atonement in Literature and Life*. Boston: Houghton, Mifflin, 1906.

Dunn, James D. G. *Jesus, Paul and the Law: Studies in Mark and Galatians*. Louisville: Westminster/John Knox, 1990.

———. *The Theology of Paul the Apostle*. Grand Rapids: Eerdmans, 1998.

———. *Romans*, vols. 38a & 38b. Word Bible Commentary. Dallas: Word, 1988.

Evans, Patricia. *The Verbally Abusive Relationship*. Avon, MS: Adams Media, 2010.

Flood, Derek. "Substitutionary Atonement and the Church Fathers: A Reply to the Authors of Pierced for Our Transgressions." *Evangelical Quarterly* 82.2 (2010), 142–59.

Forsyth, P.T. *The Work of Christ*. London: Collins, 1965.

Frankl, Viktor. *Man's Search for Meaning*. Boston: Beacon, 1959.

Girard, René. *Things Hidden Since the Foundation of the World*. New York: Althone, 1987.

———. In Brian McDonald, "Violence & the Lamb Slain: An Interview with René Girard" *Touchstone* 16.10 (Dec 2003). No pages. Online: http://www.touchstonemag.com/archives/article.php?id=16-10-040-i.

Gorman, Michael. *Cruciformity*. Grand Rapids: Eerdmans, 2001.

———. *Inhabiting the Cruciform God*. Grand Rapids: Eerdmans, 2009.

Green, Joel. *Salvation*. St. Louis: Chalice, 2003.

———. *The Theology of the Gospel of Luke*. Cambridge: Cambridge University Press, 1995.

Gregory of Nazianzus. *Fourth Theological Oration*. In *Nicene and Post Nicene Fathers, Second Series*, vol. 7. Edited by Philip Schaff & Henry Wace, 309–18. Peabody, MA: Hendrickson, 1999.

———. *Oration 40*. In *Nicene and Post Nicene Fathers, Second Series*, vol. 7. Edited by Philip Schaff and Henry Wace, 360–78. Peabody, MA: Hendrickson, 1999.

———. *To Cledonius Against Apollinaris*. In *Christology of the Later Fathers*. Edited by Edward R. Hardy, 215–24. Philadelphia: Westminster, 1954.

Gunton, Colin. *The Actuality of Atonement: A Study of Metaphor, Rationality, and the Christian Tradition*. Grand Rapids: Eerdmans, 1989.

Hall, Douglas John. *The Cross in Our Context*. Minneapolis: Fortress, 2003.

Hanson, A. T. *The Wrath of the Lamb*. London : S.P.C.K., 1957.

Hardy, Edward. *The Library of Christian Classics, Ichthus Edition: Christology of the Later Fathers*. Philadelphia: Westminster, 1954.

von Harnack, Adolf. *Outlines of the History of Dogma*. Translated by Edwin K. Mitchell. New York: Funk & Wagnalls, 1893.

Hays, Richard B. *The Moral Vision of the New Testament*. San Francisco: HarperSanFrancisco, 1996.

Hengel, Martin. *Crucifixion in the Ancient World and the "Folly" of the Message of the Cross*. Philadelphia: Fortress, 1977.

Hooker, Morna. *From Adam To Christ*. Cambridge: Cambridge University Press, 1990.

———. *The Letter to the Philippians*. The New Interpreters Bible. Nashville: Abingdon, 2000.

———. *Paul: A Short Introduction*. Oxford : Oneworld, 2003.

Irenaeus, *Against Heresies* in *Ante-Nicene Fathers*, vol. 1. Translated by Alexander Roberts. Edinburgh: T. & T. Clark, 1868.

Kähler, Martin. *The So-Called Historical Jesus and the Historic Biblical Christ*. Philadelphia: Fortress, 1964.

King, Martin Luther, Jr. "Speech at Oakwood College in Huntsville Alabama, March 2, 1962." In *King Came Preaching*. Edited by Mervyn A. Warren, 170–81. Downers Grove, IL: InterVarsity, 2001.

Loader, William. *Jesus and the Fundamentalism of His Day*. Grand Rapids: Eerdmans, 2001.

Luther, Martin. *Luther's Works*. Edited by Jaroslav Pelikan et al. St Louis: Concordia Publishing House, 1999.

———. *Luthers Werke (Weimar Ausgabe)*. D. Martin Luthers Werke, Kritische Gesamtausgabe. Weimar, 1883–.

Mackintosh, H.R. *The Christian Experience of Forgiveness*. New York: Harper & Brothers, 1927.

Marshall, Christopher D. *Beyond Retribution: A New Testament Vision for Justice, Crime, and Punishment*. Grand Rapids: Eerdmans, 2001.

McGrath, Alister. *Luther's Theology of the Cross: Martin Luther's Theological Breakthrough*. Grand Rapids: Baker, 1995.

Meyendorff, John. *Christ in Eastern Christian Thought*. Crestwood, NY: St. Vladimir's Seminary Press, 1975.

Migliore, Daniel. *Faith Seeking Understanding*. Grand Rapids: Eerdmans, 2004.

Moltmann, Jürgen. *The Crucified God: The Cross of Christ and the Foundation and Criticism of Christian Theology*. Minneapolis: Fortress, 1993.

Morris, Leon. *Apostolic Preaching of the Cross*. London: Tyndale, 1965.

Olson, Roger E. *The Mosaic of Christian Beliefs: Twenty Centuries of Unity & Diversity*. Downers Grove, IL: InterVarsity, 2002.

Packer, James I. "What Did the Cross Achieve: The Logic of Penal Substitution." In *The Collected Shorter Writings of J. I. Packer, Volume 1: Celebrating the Saving Work of God*, 85–123. Carlisle: Paternoster, 1998.

Schrage, Wolfgang. "Heil und Heilung im Neuen Testament." In *Kreuzestheologie und Ethik im Neuen Testament: Gesammelte Studien*, 87–106. Göttingen: Vandenhoeck & Ruprecht, 2004.

Sittser, Gerald. *A Grace Disguised: How the Soul Grows through Loss*. Grand Rapids: Zondervan, 2002.

Smith, Christian. *American Evangelicalism: Embattled and Thriving*. Chicago: University of Chicago Press, 1998.

Solszhenitsyn, Aleksandr. *The Gulag Archipelago*. New York: Harper Perennial, 2002.

Spurgeon, Charles. *All of Grace*. Chicago: Moody, 1974.

Stassen, Glen. *Just Peacemaking: Transforming Initiatives for Justice and Peace*. Louisville: Westminster/John Knox, 1998.

Stott, John R. W. *The Cross of Christ*. Downers Grove, IL: Intervarsity, 1986.

Walker, Lenore. *The Battered Woman Syndrome*. New York: Springer, 2009.

Weaver, J. Denney. "Atonement for the Non-Constantinian Church." *Modern Theology*, 6 (July 1990), 307–23.

———. *The Nonviolent Atonement. Second Edition, Greatly Revised and Expanded*. Grand Rapids: Eerdmans, 2001.

Wink, Walter. *Engaging the Powers*. Minneapolis: Fortress, 1992.

Wright, N.T. "The Cross and the Caricatures: A response to Robert Jenson, Jeffrey John, and a new volume entitled Pierced for Our Transgressions." *Fulcrum* (2007). No pages. Online: http://www.fulcrum-anglican.org.uk/?205.

———. *Jesus and the Victory of God*. Minneapolis: Fortress, 1996.

———. "The Letter to the Romans." *The New Interpreter's Bible: Acts–1 Corinthians*, vol. 10; Nashville: Abingdon Press, 2002.

———. *The New Testament and the People of God*. Minneapolis: Fortress, 1992.

Yancey, Philip. *What's So Amazing About Grace?* Grand Rapids: Zondervan, 1997.

Yeung, Maureen W. *Faith in Jesus and Paul*. Tübingen: Mohr Siebeck, 2002.

Zehr, Howard, *Changing Lenses: A New Focus for Crime and Justice*. Scottdale, PA: Herald, 2005.

Author Index

Author Index

Scripture Index

Subject Index

CPSIA information can be obtained
at www.ICGtesting.com
Printed in the USA
BVHW04*2335240518
517308BV00005B/10/P

9 781498 215282